"Pride, Integrity, Service" is the motto of the United States Park Rangers and Bruce Bytnar is regarded as one of the finest examples of the competence and commitment for which the men and women of the ranger force are famous.

Highly skilled in a variety of disciplines, his career took him from assignments as varied as firefighting across the western mountains to VIP protection details in eastern cities to rescue mission in the rugged Appalachians to tracking criminals through forests and fields and finally to the response in the nation's capital after the attacks of September 11.

Bytnar captures the many facets of *rangering* with the humor and insight of a master storyteller and paints the picture of life inside "the best idea we ever had" our national parks.

—*John Garrison, Former Chief Ranger of the Blue Ridge Parkway*

A Park Ranger's Life

Thirty-two Years Protecting
Our National Parks

Bruce W. Bytnar

A Park Ranger's Life:
Thirty-two Years Protecting Our National Parks

Published by Wheatmark®
610 East Delano Street, Suite 104
Tucson, Arizona 85705 U.S.A.
www.wheatmark.com

International Standard Book Number: 978-1-60494-345-0
Library of Congress Control Number: 2009934664

Cover photo by Jeremy Leadbetter

For Linda and Brian
Thanks for sharing the life of a
national park ranger

Contents

Preface

A t an early age most children are asked, "What do you want to be when you grow up?" I am sure I went through the usual stages of cowboy, fireman, and such. But my earliest memory of an answer to this question was "A park ranger." This may have been influenced by my parents exposing me at an early age to national parks. We visited many historic sites and parks in the east, and that is where I first met park rangers, in their green and gray uniforms and large, flat hats. One of these experiences was at Gettysburg National Military Park, where I first witnessed a ranger astride a horse patrolling the battlefield, helping to protect our national heritage. This planning for my future was further influenced by years of my youth spent outdoors roaming old, untended fields and woods surrounding our suburban home in Maryland. I was later privileged to have several adult mentors while in the Boy Scouts, who encouraged me in living an active life of adventure and public service.

Many years later, while attending college and majoring in parks and recreation management, I signed up for a course entitled "Introduction to Interpretive Services." When I showed up for the first day of class, I was excited to find that the guest instructor was Tom Westmoreland, the chief ranger at Fort McHenry National Monument in Baltimore, Maryland. My participation in this class started an association with Tom that resulted in my first job as a seasonal park ranger at Fort McHenry in 1975. From Tom Westmoreland I learned of the mission of the National Park Service and the dedication that it takes to meet the expectations of those inspiring words.

The first national park was Yellowstone, established in 1872. I am able to put this in some historical perspective when I think about how that was just seven years after the American Civil War ended. Following that time, the early parks were managed and patrolled by the U.S. Army. Today the Yellowstone National Park headquarters is located in the old Army cavalry post that was once established to protect the park and its early visitors.

By 1916 it was realized that an agency of resource professionals was needed to better manage this growing idea of national parks. It was in that year that the National Park Service was established by the *Organic Act*, which stated that the mission of the National Park Service shall be "to conserve the scenery and natural and historic objects and the wildlife therein and to provide for the enjoyment of the same in such manner and by such means as will leave them unimpaired for the enjoyment of future generations."

In 1983 Wallace Stegner, American historian, writer, and environmentalist, wrote, "National parks are the best idea we ever had. Absolutely American, absolutely democratic, they reflect us at our best rather than our worst."

Today the National Park Service is responsible for areas as diverse as the Statue of Liberty and Yosemite National Park; the Great Smokey Mountains and the Mall in Washington, D.C.; Martin Luther King, Jr.'s, birthplace and Hawaii volcanoes. No matter what national park area you may visit, one constant is the park ranger. They are the ones charged with that mission of so long ago to preserve and protect our nation's heritage for future generations.

The significance and importance for our future of the national parks was imbedded in my entire being during this period. At Fort McHenry I decided to make the mission of the National Park Service my life's work. Those basics that I learned while working for Tom Westmoreland carried me in good stead throughout my career.

I was fortunate to eventually return to Fort McHenry for my first permanent job with the National Park Service in March 1977. Later that same year, I transferred to a ranger position at Fredericksburg and Spotsylvania National Military Park. I worked there in a protection position until 1981, when I transferred to the Blue Ridge Parkway in North Carolina. During my time on the Parkway, I worked in three different districts, ending my career in 2008 as the Ridge District ranger in Virginia.

During this time I served as a commissioned federal law enforcement officer, structural and wildland firefighter, natural and historical resource interpreter, search and rescue manager, emergency medical technician, instructor and mentor, public health inspector, incident commander, park planner, supervisor, and manager. A national park ranger wears many hats that can change many times during even one day. I served on extended details in many national park areas and fought fires in Idaho, Montana, California, Utah, Oregon, Virginia, Florida, North Carolina, Maryland, and Pennsylvania.

Every national park ranger has stories. In fact, at any gathering of park rangers you will find somewhere off in a corner several storytellers trying to top each other. What follows are a collection of my stories reflecting my experiences during more than thirty-two years as a national park ranger. In most cases the names of people involved have been changed to protect not only the innocent, but also the guilty and myself.

"What Is It You Do?"

I have found that while on duty in our national parks, the most frequently asked question (after "Where is the restroom?") is "What does a park ranger do?" This leads one to believe there is definitely a common thread of interest among the public about the mysterious ways of rangers. It is easy to say that a park ranger does a little bit of everything or is a jack of all trades, but I am not sure that these colloquialisms really cover it.

"Hey ranger, boy I always wanted to be a park ranger. By the way, what is it you do all day?"

"Gee, I wish I had a job just riding around up out here all day. Is that what you guys do all the time?"

"Hey, ranger, how is Smokey the Bear doing?"

When I would get questions like these, it would not bother me to sit down and try to explain what my job entailed. The problem was that most people did not have the time or the patience to really get the full answer. Any park ranger worth a grain of salt can make at least an hour's dissertation out of this one inquiry if his or her creative juices are flowing. Over the years I have attempted numerous techniques and explanations of this perplexing informational need. These answers range from bad days where I want to say, "Yeah, I love riding around up here at your expense, and by the way, your dog needs to be on a leash," to the good days when I make the effort to sit down with someone and really try to explain my life so they will understand and leave with the strong opinion that rangers are the closest thing to Superman and are grossly underpaid.

I recall the time that I was patrolling the Blue Ridge Parkway when I pulled into an overlook and discovered that one of the local farmer's cattle had gotten out of the pasture the night before. Although the cattle were gone, they had left evidence of their dalliance in the park by leaving behind about fifty cow pies. I sat there, thinking that it was Friday afternoon, the maintenance crew had gone home, and it was the beginning of a busy fall color season weekend. Well, I sat there for a minute or two and examined the situation thoroughly. (No ranger makes a move without the benefit of thorough examination.) With this step out of the way, I then got my fire shovel out of my car's trunk and started relocating the natural fertilizer to the laurel and rhododendron plants below the overlook. I was about halfway through my task, and making slow progress, when a vehicle pulled into the overlook. I was standing there with a shovelful of fertilizer when a young man with an enthusiastic grin on his face jumped out of the passenger side and ran up to me. Based on his exigent exit of the vehicle, I was expecting him to either report some type of life-threatening horrendous emergency or ask the location of the nearest bathroom, and I was already processing what my answer might be. I just stood there holding onto my shovelful of cow pie, and he approached and asked exuberantly, "Gee, I always wanted to be a park ranger. What do you guys do?" I looked him in the eye, glanced at my shovel, then back at him and simply responded, "A little bit of everything, just a little bit of everything."

The next day I left for a special detail to Mammoth Cave National Park to assist in providing protection for then President Ronald Reagan's visit to the park. This is just one example of how park rangers change gears quickly to meet a wide variety of duties and challenges.

You never know what is going to happen next in a national park. No matter how you plan your day, it never turns out that way. Many times, planned activities are interrupted by emergencies and problems ranging from motor vehicle accidents, fires, illegal hunting, lost visitors, or wildlife mixing with people. I remember one incident when a ranger was conducting an evening campfire program showing slides to an audience of over one hundred visitors. Suddenly, they were interrupted by a man covered with blood, who ran in front of the group, lighted by the projector, screaming for help. Most people initially thought it was part of the program. When the ranger followed the man out to his vehicle, she found a second man who had been shot. The ranger then had to call for an ambulance, administer first aid, calm the crowd and victim, and then go back and finish the program. On top of all that, it was also the evening a supervisor had shown up to audit the program. By the way, the ranger got a good rating for her performance.

Due to the constant call for unpredictable responses to emergencies and other daily park problems, it is almost impossible to plan ahead for family or personal activities. In only a half-joking vein, my wife always left for work saying something like, "I'll be home around five." When I left I always said, "I'll be home when I can." On a Saturday in 1987, I went to work for a regular day scheduled to get off at around five thirty. As it turned out, I did not get home for about two weeks. In this case we had a search for a lost hiker who was reported to be possibly suicidal. I cannot even remember all the chores that did not get done at home during that period. Needless to say, there have also been endless numbers of uneaten dinners and unattended family events.

One symbol that people often associate with rangers is the mascot Smokey the Bear. By the way, Smokey actually belongs to the U.S. Forest Service, not the National Park Service, but even we have a hard time keeping that straight. When I gave presentations at schools on forest fire prevention and firefighting, children always ask where Smokey is and if he fights fires with me. I have to admit that I never have actually seen Smokey on a fire, but I have been told he is usually around. Fighting forest fires throughout the country was an activity in which I was heavily involved during my career. Not only are rangers responsible for responding to fires in the area where they are assigned, but they are also subject to calls for fires throughout the United States. The National Park Service is part of the Interagency Wildfire System, and employees remain on call for emergencies throughout the country. These assignments usually meant being away from home for periods of two to three weeks. Your notification that you are going on a fire normally ranges from forty-eight to twelve hours before you have to be at the airport, ready to go. My family usually loves it when one of these assignments pops up. One year my wife and I were being good relatives and offered to take my brother-in-law's three daughters for a week. The second day they were at our house, I was called for a fire detail in Oregon, and my wife ended up with the expanded solo parental detail. Another time while I was gone, our basement flooded, and we have also had two of our family dogs die while I was away. Needless to say, I get a bit nervous about leaving on any last-minute trips.

One night I was sitting in my nice, cozy living room watching television with my wife when I got a phone call that there was a car broken down in the middle of the road about three miles from our home on the Blue Ridge Parkway. I put on my uniform and equipment and left, responding in my patrol car. I was surprised to find that even though it was April I had to wipe the freshly fallen snow from my windshield. I drove up the parkway and found a 1968 Ford Mustang sitting in the middle of the southbound lane. I walked up to the car and could see that there were several persons huddled inside. By this time the snow was really starting to blow. I wiped some snow from the driver's side window and called to the driver. He did not answer so I gently tapped on the window. He looked up but still did not respond. I could see some discussion going on between at least three occupants. I tapped again, not so gently this time, on the window, and the driver finally rolled it open just enough to speak through it. I asked him what the problem was, and he told me the transmission was out on his car. I informed him that I would try to get a wrecker for him. When I got back to my car, I started to once again thoroughly examine the situation and remembered that just before leaving the house I had been watching the TV news on the one snowy channel we could get. There was a report about four prisoners escaping from a large city's jail about two hours from where I was. I called the license plate of the car into our dispatcher, and it did not come back as a stolen or wanted car. I then went back to the Mustang and asked the driver for his license. He told me that he had forgotten it at home. I asked if anyone else in the car had any identification. Finally one of the passengers in the back seat gave me a draft card. Now, I thought that was downright suspicious in itself, and I felt sure something was going on and that I did not yet have the full story.

I returned again to my car and gave the dispatcher the name on the draft card. I then requested her to contact the police in the city where the prison escape had occurred. When she called me back I could tell she was excited by the fact that her voice was at least two octaves higher than before. She had discovered that the name on the draft card was that of one of the prisoners who had escaped and that the car had been stolen but the police had not yet had time to enter the vehicle's information into the computer. I then requested that the dispatcher contact the state police to ask for some help in transporting the occupants of the car. I called out to the vehicle with the public address speaker my patrol car and eventually got them to step out of their car into the falling snow, which was beginning to look a lot more like a blizzard. After searching each of the three occupants at gun point, I searched the interior of the car. There I found several weapons, including a handgun and a butcher knife. By this time the snow was really picking up and the temperature was dropping. None of the prisoners had coats on, and they were beginning to shiver, so I put them back into their car. I then stood outside by my vehicle with a shotgun watching them, waiting for backup to arrive. I figured that help should be there within about forty minutes. Almost two hours later a county deputy arrived. I learned later that the state police had wrecked two cars trying to get to me in the snow. I remember finally getting back into my car and leaning over to answer the radio and having about four inches of snow fall off my hat, covering the radio and center console of the car.

These are just a few examples of the types of duties rangers may be called upon to perform at a moment's notice. On a daily basis throughout the nearly four hundred areas managed by the National Park Service, rangers risk their lives to save others and protect the resources of our parks.

Today you will find the rangers attempting to maintain the high ideals of the agency's mission through many different techniques, including education of the public about the resources in a park, scientific research and monitoring of fragile resources, patrolling the parks to make them safe, responding to life-threatening emergencies, preventing and fighting fires, and investigating and prosecuting violators of laws and regulations.

National Park Service Basics

To aid the reader in understanding some of the stories that follow, a basic knowledge of the National Park Service and how it works may help. The National Park Service (the NPS) is an agency of the federal government. These are the same people that brought you the Internal Revenue Service, Social Security Administration, Medicare, and many other hard–to–understand bureaucracies. Titles, structures, and chain of command can be quite confusing to those who have not spent their lives working for the government.

The National Park Service is an agency within the executive branch of government under the Department of the Interior. A director who works out of the main Interior building in Washington, D.C., is a presidential appointee charged with overall administration and management of the almost four hundred units of the National Park Service stretching from Guam in the Pacific to the American Virgin Islands. All these parks are divided into seven areas overseen by regional offices. The individual park units fall under each regional director.

A national park unit is managed by a superintendent, who has overall responsibility for all operations of the unit under their supervision. These units range from national parks to historic sites, seashores, monuments, and parkways. The size, complexity, and level of staffing within the park unit determine its organization and distribution of jobs.

The basic national park staff organization is focused on the functions of

- Protection—This includes the jobs of law enforcement, fire-fighting, public safety, visitor management, campground management, public health inspections, search and rescue, and emergency medical services.

- Interpretation—This is the education job that includes presenting guided walks and programs centering on the resources of the park. Also included in this job is running visitor centers, managing exhibit and display design, holding outreach programs in schools, writing brochures, and maintaining websites.

- Maintenance—Here you will find the employees tasked with keeping the park clean, safe, and prepared for visitors. Here you will also find engineers, architects, sanitarians, radio technicians, and more service positions. Work involving construction is conducted by this division.

- Administration—These people keep the budget straight, take care of employee hiring and benefit practices, keep the computers running, and conduct purchasing and contracting for the park.

- Resource Management—Here you find the scientists and historians responsible for monitoring, researching, and making recommendations for practices to best protect both cultural and natural resources.

Most national park areas have their staff divided in some semblance of these functions. The chief ranger works directly under the superintendent and supervises protection and in smaller parks the interpretive park rangers. Larger parks are divided into geographic districts, with each having a supervisor with the title of district ranger.

The basic requirement to become a national park ranger is a four-year college degree. There are no specific degree requirements. I have worked with park rangers that have degrees in nuclear physics, history, biology, parks and recreation management, Russian studies, resources management, English, geography, and many more. The large number of people applying for full-time national park employment make the competition quite difficult. Most park rangers start their careers working as temporary seasonal employees, working up to six-month periods without benefits of health insurance or retirement investment. When working in the seasonal ranks, many people move around the country from job to job, as funding and time run out. Although this is tough on establishing a regular life or family, a person can develop work experience and valuable contacts that aid in their achieving a full-time permanent position. I worked as a seasonal employee for three years before obtaining a permanent position at Fort McHenry National Monument and Historic Shrine in Baltimore, Maryland.

Not all park rangers are law enforcement officers. Under the Authorities Act, the secretary of the interior may authorize specific employees as commissioned federal law enforcement officers. Rangers in these positions attend basic law enforcement instruction at the Federal Law Enforcement Training Center in Brunswick, Georgia. Here park rangers train alongside all other federal law enforcement agencies, (excluding the FBI). These rangers also must be able to pass medical standards and physical fitness testing twice a year. Federal background investigations that show clean criminal histories are also required.

This information should assist the reader in understanding some of the experiences of working in national parks. What follows are brief descriptions of the national park areas where I have worked and which will serve as the backdrop for my stories.

Fort McHenry

I was hired for my first temporary seasonal job with the National Park Service at Fort McHenry National Monument and Historic Shrine in Baltimore, Maryland, in June 1975. My official job title was a GS-3 Park Aid, and I made $3.15 an hour. This did not sound very romantic or exciting, but I was to be uniformed as and perform the duties of a national park ranger. I was thrilled beyond belief. A childhood dream was coming true. I will never forget the thrill when my first uniforms arrived from the Gregory's Company in California. I had received a uniform allowance check that covered about a third of the cost for the required initial uniforms for the job. I could feel my heart rate increase as I opened the box and put my first Stetson flat hat (the traditional ranger hat, or what some call "Smokey the Bear hat") on my head and stared into the mirror.

Fort McHenry is a masonry fortification built as part of the defenses of Baltimore Harbor. Construction of the original fort was started in 1776, and it remained an active army post until 1933. It came into fame during the War of 1812, when, following the burning of our young nation's capital at Washington, the British army and naval forces attacked Baltimore. The battle was observed by a Maryland attorney named Francis Scott Key, who was being held on one of the British ships. His sight of the giant flag still standing over Fort McHenry after twenty-two hours of bombardment by mortars and rockets inspired him to write our country's anthem, the "Star Spangled Banner." That original flag can be seen today at the Smithsonian Institution in Washington, D.C.

Today the park includes more than forty-two grassed acres in the middle of one of the largest industrial ports in the world. This oasis of green surrounded by heavy industrial urban landscape includes a modern visitor's center in addition to the original brick fort that withstood the British attack in 1814.

Fredericksburg and Spotsylvania National Military Park

In September 1977 I packed up my new wife, who had to resign from her teaching job, and transferred to Fredericksburg and Spotsylvania National Military Park in Virginia. I remained a GS-4 with no promotion, but this opportunity moved me to a larger park with a variety of duties.

The name of this park was long and difficult to trip off the tongue, so it had the nickname of Fred Spot. The geographic location of this park, directly between Washington, D.C., and Richmond, Virginia, made it one of the most hotly contested pieces of real estate during the Civil War. Whereas most Civil War battlefields preserved by the National Park Service commemorate one single event or conflict, this park had four major battles fought on its soil. These were the battles of Fredericksburg in 1862, Chancellorsville in 1863, and the Wilderness and Spotsylvania Courthouse Battles in 1864.

The park is divided into separate units, with private property breaking it into locations spread through three counties and the city of Fredericksburg. There are over 30 miles of roads within the park, but to drive them all you need to drive almost

125 miles on state and county roads that connect the battle-fields.

There are many historic structures protected within the park, some dating back to the colonial period before the battles occurred. Many of the original trenches and gun emplacements constructed during the Civil War are also found within the park's boundaries. These structures mark the areas where military units were placed and where our forefathers fought and died.

The Blue Ridge Parkway

In January 1981 my wife had to again resign from another teaching job to follow me on a transfer to the Blue Ridge Parkway in North Carolina. We moved to what was known as the Bluffs Sub-District and moved into a park residence near Laurel Springs, North Carolina. During the next twenty-eight years we moved two more times on the Blue Ridge Parkway. In 1983 we moved one hundred miles south when I was promoted to be the assistant district ranger for the Gillespie Gap District. We made a final move of three hundred miles in June 1985, when I became the James River district ranger in Virginia.

The Blue Ridge Parkway is an elongated national park stretching for 469 miles through the eastern edge of the Appalachian Mountains in Virginia and North Carolina. The park was established in 1935 to connect the Great Smokey Mountains and Shenandoah national parks. It stretches along mountain ridges, high elevation habitats, plateaus, and valleys. The ever-changing views reflect the Southern Appalachian geography and its effects on the society that has developed within its shadows.

Most think of the Blue Ridge Parkway as just a long, scenic ribbon of roadway. I admit this was my opinion before working there. In truth, it is much more than that. The park could be described as a long rope with many large knots tied in it. The knots represent the large tracts of protected lands along its route that preserve native habitats, cultural landscapes and structures, and recreational opportunities centered on outdoor activities. The Blue Ridge Parkway averages nineteen million visitors a year, which results in many challenges of balancing the enjoyment of the public with the preservation and protection of irreplaceable resources.

When I first moved to the Blue Ridge Parkway, my wife and I planned on a two- to three-year stay before moving on to an even more exciting assignment out west. What we discovered was a region, a park, and people that we felt we would never be able to find anywhere else. I found that career–wise, there was nothing else a park ranger could want. The park was busy year-round and challenged all the skills that could be developed by a national park ranger. Our love affair with the mountains, their coves, and streams took hold and kept us from wanderlust. We put down our roots.

Interesting People

With Fort McHenry located in the middle of a major city with a greatly diverse population, it was inevitable that many interesting people would stop by the park. After all, entry to Fort McHenry was then free. The park is located at the end of the city bus line on Fort Avenue, and often we would meet people that had just ridden quite figuratively to the end of the line.

Tattoo Tillie

One of the best known or notorious characters we often met was known as Tattoo Tillie. No one knew her real name. She was most likely homeless and always intoxicated when she came to the park. She got her nickname from her regular attendance at the tattoo ceremonies held weekly in the fort during the summer. Each week, the U.S. Marine Corps Marching Band and a platoon of marines in their dress blues would come to the park and recreate a formal tattoo. This was a military tradition that occurred prior to "Taps" or last call on military posts during the eighteenth and nineteenth centuries. Each week a dignitary was invited to be the "honorary colonel" and review the troops. It was quite an impressive show that drew large crowds.

In addition to the marines each week we always had a visit from Tattoo Tillie. Her level of intoxication would determine how she would disrupt the evening. One time she faked a fall on the walkway and had the rescue crew that was standing by load her in the ambulance. They caught her trying to grab a bottle of rubbing alcohol behind their backs and threw her out of the ambulance. She then stomped off, miraculously cured shouting obscenities back over her shoulder.

Another of her antics was to stop wherever she was and, no matter who was around, lift her skirt, squat, and pee in front of the world. This was usually followed by loud expletives directed at anyone caught gaping in surprise.

One day I was in the fort, having just finished leading a guided tour, when a frantic intercom call came in from the visitor center. Apparently there was a woman passed out in the theater, and the person at the desk did not know what to do. I went to see what I could do to help. I entered the front of the theater, since there were no movies showing at the time, and found Tattoo Tillie passed out in the front row. At the rear of the small theater were eight or ten visitors who had been ushered in to view the next showing of the park introductory film. I could see expectation in their eyes, wondering what I was going to do. The real show was about to begin. At that moment, Ernie, one of the maintenance workers who had been at Fort McHenry seemingly forever, walked in. I was grabbing for straws at that point and asked if he knew this woman's name.

He proudly answered in an overly dramatic and loud voice, "Of course I know her name."

No further information appeared to be forthcoming, so I asked, "Well, what's her name?"

In an even louder stage voice, he proclaimed, "Why, that's Tattoo Tillie." I suddenly realized that I had been expecting information from the same genius who had been recently arrested for showing pornographic films at his home by using his window's shades for a screen. Apparently this spectacle had drawn quite a crowd on the sidewalk in front of his local neighborhood row house.

I stood there dumbstruck, having expected some type of more helpful information. I looked across at the small crowd of visitors who at this point were riveted in their seats, not wanting to miss the next act in this drama unfolding before them.

I could see that the woman was breathing deeply and appeared to be asleep, or more likely she was passed out, as was evident from the odor of cheap, alcoholic beverages about her person. I then leaned forward and shook her shoulder, being careful not to upset her from her seat. As I shook her, I called to her with the only name I knew, "Tattoo, Tattoo." The single response I got was a muffled grump as she pulled the bag in her lap tighter.

I once again looked across at the visitors who were all now sitting with large grins on their faces. I could tell they were enjoying the performance. I knew the Baltimore police or fire departments would have nothing to do with our guest, so being at a loss for what to do next, I officiously informed Tattoo Tillie's fellow theatergoers that she was harmless and that they would be safe. They all laughed and said she had not been bothering anyone.

I then went back to the lady working at our front desk and told her to just leave Tattoo Tillie alone, and that eventually she would wake up and leave. If there was a problem, she should call me, and I would try to take care of it. I learned later that Tillie had slept through three showings of the introductory film and then staggered out of the theater, out of the visitor center, and out of the park. That was the last time I ever saw Tattoo Tillie. I have often wondered, but not too often, whatever happened to her.

The Bicycle Man

Another regular visitor to the park was known as the Bicycle Man. He was a mentally challenged adult who, during my time at Fort McHenry, was in his late thirties. He lived with his parents in the neighborhood outside the park and contributed to making his way by washing police cars and ambulances. Officers from the local precinct would pull up to his house, and he would wash their cars and be paid in cash. I always thought it was a nice gesture on the part of the police and fire departments.

Most of the park staff did not really know how to react to the Bicycle Man. His speech was not very clear, and he spoke loudly. It was easy for him to become upset and become even louder if confronted or questioned. As a result, most people avoided and ignored him.

The other challenge of dealing with the Bicycle Man was that each time he came to the park he was a different fictional character. This was part of the reason I never learned his real name. Not only would he tell you who he was on that day, but he also dressed the part and decorated his bicycle to match. The characters I remember most were Popeye the Sailor, Tom Mix, Dick Tracy, and Roy Rogers. Most people would just shake their heads and say, "Okay," and then walk away from him.

One day I came across the Bicycle Man dressed in full sailor hat, bell-bottom sailor pants, with a plastic anchor and chain hanging around his bicycle handlebar. He was sitting on a retaining wall in front of the visitor center with his head hanging low and was almost in tears. People were just walking by, giving him a sideways glance, and then pretending he was not there. One of the other park staff members had seen him earlier and told me that he was telling people that he was Popeye the Sailor that day. It tore at my heart to see this down-trodden but good person so full of obvious despair. So I walked up to him and said, "What's wrong, Popeye?"

He immediately looked up at me, with his sailor hat sitting rakishly on his head, and piped up, "Do you believe I am Popeye?"

I said, "Sure, if you say so."

His face lit up, and he stretched out his had to shake mine. I purposely took a dramatic pause and asked him, "If you have been eating your spinach, just don't squeeze my hand to hard." He grinned and gave me a big firm, but not too firm, handshake, then turned and grabbed his bike. I asked him where he was going. "Got to go home," was his reply, and he took off toward the gate to the park.

After that, whenever he came to the park, he looked for me and would come up to tell me who he was that day. I would greet him as his character; he would grin and then just go off, happy as a lark. Like all of us, I think he just needed some recognition from another human being.

The Ex-Chief Ranger

Within the grounds of Fort McHenry were two small 1950s-style rambler houses. One was occupied by the park superintendent, the other by the chief ranger. One day the chief ranger's wife, Martha, was in the tiny backyard hanging out the laundry when she heard some movement in the bushes. When she approached she found a man hiding, watching her. Now most people, let alone a woman startled in her own backyard, would have panicked and run or even screamed upon such a discovery, but Martha was a very calm, controlled woman who grew up in Texas and had spent many years living in national parks. She just looked at the man and asked, "What are you doing?"

He stood up, looked her in the eye, and replied, "I was just checking to see who is living in my house." With that he simply walked away through the maintenance area and out into the city. Martha thought this a bit odd and called her husband, Tom, at the office. Tom took this a little more seriously and immediately attempted to locate the guy but with no success. Later, one of the older maintenance workers came forward and told Tom that he had seen the man looking through the maintenance area earlier and recognized him as Bill Browning, a previous chief ranger at Fort McHenry.

Over the next few days, and quite a few phone calls and interviews of long-term employees, a picture of who Bill Browning was came together.

Bill was a ranger in a remote western park for many years. It is not clear what went on there, but his supervisors felt that he had some serious problems, and the decision was made to move him to a more urban area. For some reason, they thought that this would be the solution. It would also get him out of their hair. So Bill came to Baltimore, to be the chief ranger at Fort McHenry.

It did not take long for people to notice some odd things

about Bill. When he came to work in the mornings, he walked across a grassed area approximately four hundred yards to the office. Each day he wore two guns, one on each hip, and upon arriving he would take them off and put them in a safe. At lunchtime he would put the guns back on to walk home; then, returning to work after lunch, once again he placed the guns back in the safe. At the end of the day he put the guns on and went home. He never wore the guns anywhere else in the park and never mentioned or discussed them with anyone. This was during a time period when National Park Service management strongly frowned on rangers wearing guns, and no one at this park had ever worn one gun, let alone two.

Then one day, yelling was heard from the chief ranger's house. When people arrived, they found Bill on the roof in a full karate outfit, yelling incoherently and making karate moves. He would not respond to anyone who attempted to talk to him. Bill's wife was in the house, and when she was checked on, it became apparent that she had been beaten. It took several park employees with the help of the Baltimore Police Department to physically remove Bill from the roof. He was then taken off for psychiatric evaluation but returned to the park wearing his two guns the next morning.

Next to the park is a city fireboat station. This facility was manned twenty-four hours a day, seven days a week, by a complete crew. Their building was located at the pier, which held their tugboat-like ship. The fireboat station building was up against an ornate iron rail fence separating it from the park. The space between the widow of their dispatcher's desk and this fence was only two feet.

Late one night, when most of the crew was in bed upstairs, the one awake dispatcher at the desk heard, "Psst, Pssst" from outside the open window. When he stuck his head out he observed a man dressed in a karate outfit on the other side of the fence in the park.

The karate-clad man asked in a conspiratorial tone, "Hey, will you get me a Coke?"

The soft drink machine was located upstairs in the crew's

kitchen area. The dispatcher responded, "I am on duty and I can't leave the radio desk."

The man said, "Oh, come on. You can get me a Coke. It will only take a minute."

Again the dispatcher tried to explain that he could not leave the desk. The karate man then became agitated and cursed at the fireman, eventually disappearing into the dark.

Less than five minutes later, the front door of the fireboat station flew open, throwing the double door back against the walls, almost popping them off their hinges. In ran the karate clad man, Bill Browning, this time armed with a large, and what appeared to be sharp, axe. Before the dispatcher sitting behind his panel in the corner of the room could react, Bill (who in legend would became known as the "Mad Axe Man of Fort McHenry") attacked the pool table located in the middle of the large, open room. Once he had sufficiently damaged that, he turned his energy on the antique alarm bell system mounted to the wall.

Between the axe man yelling, the dispatcher screaming for help, and the sounds of damage being done by the axe, the dozen or so firemen upstairs finally awoke from their slumber and poured down the stairs. Surrounding the culprit, they were able to talk him down and get the axe away from him without anyone getting hurt. The Baltimore Police Department was summoned, and Bill Browning, the mad axe man, was taken to the local precinct. There, he was subjected to a psychiatric evaluation and eventually transferred to a state mental hospital for treatment.

It was not until the next day that the Fort McHenry staff was notified that their chief ranger, Bill Browning, had been arrested the night before. Bill was eventually terminated from his job and placed in the extended care of the State of Maryland.

In 1977, there was a media blitz on state mental hospitals, and various stories appeared about patients being kept for no real reason and costing the taxpayers exorbitant amounts of money for care. A public outcry arose to release many of these "unjustly" confined people. Hundreds of marginally ill people were released, and this included Bill Browning. He had been out for a few weeks and was living at the YMCA in downtown Baltimore. Bill started to show up at the park, telling people that he was going to get his job back. He told the chief ranger's wife on their second meeting that she should start packing her bags, because he wanted his house back.

Since I had some success in dealing with the likes of Tattoo Tillie and the Bicycle Man, my fellow employees wanted me to be the one to talk to Bill Browning when he showed up. At first, he attempted to avoid me whenever he came into the park. Eventually I was able to talk to him, although he seemed very secretive and uncomfortable. I began to pity rather than fear him. He seemed to be a broken and cowed man. He did bring up in any contact that I had with him that he was going to get his job back. People noticed that he carried a small notebook and appeared to be writing all the time. He started going on the guided tours in the fort, and this really scared some staff. They were afraid he would go crazy in the middle of a crowd.

One day, he came on one of my tours. At the end, I saw him off by himself writing in his notebook. I approached him quietly and startled him when I said hello. He quickly tried to hide the notebook.

"What are you writing down there, Bill?," I asked.

"None of your business."

"I was just curious since you were just on my tour."

"Well if you must know," said Bill, "I am making notes on who I am going to keep and who I am going to fire when I get back my job as chief ranger."

"Oh, well, what about me? Are you going to let me stay on?," I said, with a note of concern in my voice.

"Oh yeah, I 'm going to let you stay," said Bill. "I like the way you talk to people, and I like your tours."

"Great, that makes me feel much better." After that, I would not say we were friends, but Bill seemed a bit more at ease around me. I was then officially assigned to him as his keeper or watcher whenever he came to the park. It got to the point that when the real chief ranger was not around and Bill showed up, some employees would call me on my day off to see if I would come in to protect them. It was not a good situation.

Once Bill somehow got behind the information desk in the visitor center and barged into the superintendent's office just before closing. Bill demanded his job back and wanted it now. The superintendent was intimidated having this crazy man in his office and said, "Bill, I don't have the authority to do that. Only the regional director in Philadelphia can do that." This was the first idea that popped into his head to get this mad man out of his office. Bill seemed to accept this and left quietly.

Within a few days the superintendent received a telephone call from the regional office. Apparently, Bill Browning showed up in Philadelphia and barged his way into the regional director's office, demanding his job back. The regional director and his staff were dumbfounded and had no idea who this man was or what his story might be. The regional director used the first defense he could think of, and told Bill that he did not have the authority to give him his job back. Only the director of the park service could do that. Bill finally left the building, escorted by the regional law enforcement specialist, a captain from the U.S. Park Police.

The superintendent was a bit shaken by this development, and the regional director was not happy that Bill Browning had been aiming for him.

No one had anticipated the determination of Bill Browning, for the next week, another call came from the Washington headquarters of the park service. After all that Bill Browning had been through, apparently no one had thought to relieve him of his government employee ID card. He used this to get into the U.S. Department of Interior building in Washington, D.C., and stormed into the office of the director of the National Park Service, once again demanding his job back. This time, the director immediately called security and had Bill removed from the building. Within an hour, Bill returned through another entrance of the building, one of the largest buildings in the city, and again barged into the directors office. This time, Bill was not only removed from the building, but he was searched and his government ID was confiscated. He was also informed by one of the director's assistants that he would never be restored to his old position and to give up this fight.

Bill returned to his YMCA room in Baltimore to continue his fight through the mail. He wrote weekly to congressmen and senators, explaining his plight and his desire to get his job back. After all, the state of Maryland and their army of doctors had given him a clean bill of health and released him from the mental institution. Each one of his letters that was sent was forwarded to Fort McHenry with a cover letter from the official contacted, wanting an explanation. Written responses were required within forty-eight hours back to the officials' offices. These eventually became form letters, and after more than a dozen enquiries, the congressional offices stopped processing Bill's requests.

During this period, Bill still kept lurking around Fort McHenry, taking his notes and watching people. The majority of the staff were paranoid about his constant presence, fearing he would once again explode into an act of violence. As the time of my transfer and promotion approached, several fellow employees became concerned that my leaving might precipitate a violent event, since I was the only one that Bill would talk to. One person even came to me one day and asked how I could leave them in such a situation.

After working almost three years in the middle of a major city rather than a more traditionally thought of national park and dealing with so many interesting people, I told them that it was easy.

I later learned that Bill Browning continued to visit the park, but as time went by his visits became less frequent and eventually ended. No one knew what finally became of him, but we assumed that he never got a job back in the National Park Service, at least as far as we knew.

The experience I gained in working with these people benefited me many times through my career. No matter how appalling or miserable a position a person may be at in their life, they still struggle, as we all do, for respect as a human being.

I learned the lesson of portraying respect to others, whether it was heartfelt or not. By acting respectfully to even the most despicable criminals I was able to gain their cooperation, and, in many instances, their stories together with confessions or information on further crimes and criminals. This concept of respect even helped in the handling of tragedies such as fatalities of visitors in our national parks. I always made it a point to show respect for human remains. It was impossible to measure the comfort this gave to family members and helped calm nervous or upset emergency workers.

Supervisory Park Technician

I was hired for my first seasonal park service job by then chief ranger Tom Westmoreland after completing a course he taught at a local community college. I was to become an interpretive ranger with responsibilities for conducting guided tours, working the information desk in the visitor center, and answering any type of questions the visitors might have. I was told we would have one week of training, followed by on-the-job experience.

What I did not know was that there had been quite a few changes in the park's administration just before I came on duty. The park had a very small full-time permanent ranger staff consisting of the chief ranger, a historian, and a supervisory park technician. The supervisory park technician was a man named Dan Weekly, a retired navy chief petty officer who for years had been sidetracked into menial jobs by previous superintendents. The reason for this would become quite apparent during my time at Fort McHenry. Dan was in his late sixties, overweight, bald, with a ruddy face and a large bulbous nose. Just going up and down the stairs made him wheeze so hard you would think he was going to have a heart attack.

A new superintendent for the park had just arrived in April, and he was convinced that Dan Weekly had been treated unjustly in the past. After all, his position carried the title "supervisory." So for the first time in the ten years Dan had worked in the Park, he was put in total charge of the new seasonal staff of twelve people, including me. For the past five years there had been a seasonal employee who worked as a teacher in Baltimore, and he came back year after year and actually supervised the seasonal and interpretive operations. He returned that year but was demoted two grades and clearly told that he was not in charge anymore.

The first day of work, all the new employees were herded into the basement of the visitor center, where there was a small meeting room. We were welcomed by the superintendent, instructed on the mission and purpose of the National Park Service by the chief ranger, and then given a lecture on the historical events that led to the writing of the "Star Spangled Banner." I found this all fascinating and ate it up. The next day we were turned over to Dan Weekly, whose job, we were told, was to turn us into interpretive rangers. It quickly became clear to us that he had no idea how to do that.

The second day, Dan, who wanted us all to call him chief after his naval rank, chased us all back into the basement. The five returning seasonal employees were left upstairs to conduct business with park visitors. We sat around for about an hour when Dan came downstairs and put us all in our place, as he would have done with new navy recruits. He let us know that we did not know how to do anything, and that he was not going to let us ruin this park. No one was permitted upstairs without his permission (that was where the restrooms were located, by the way) nor talk to any visitors. A few people started to ask him questions about what training we were going to receive. He seemed confused and then left in a huff, leaving us for two more hours.

Eventually, on our own, we started looking through bookshelves and found some materials that we could read and share among ourselves about the history of the fort. Several fellow employees were local high school history teachers, and they began to give impromptu lectures to fill the rest of us in on the important stories behind Fort McHenry.

After a week of sitting in the basement the chief ranger finally ordered Dan Weekly to get us out into the park. Dan's solution was to move us into an empty room in one of the historic buildings inside the fort itself. This room was dark and damp, with covered windows and only two bare light bulbs hanging from the exposed rafters of the ceiling. At least in being out of the visitor center, the experienced seasonal employees would come in and try to pass on some information that they thought would be pertinent to our jobs. One of our assemblage of lost souls decided to teach us how to speed-read to pass the time. A sense of rebellion was starting to take seed, and several people started to discuss quitting. But I had just started my dream job and could not believe that it could end like this. Surely, this was not what the entire National Park Service was like.

During the third week of our limbo training period, we were still sitting in the dark room in the fort. The bathrooms in the fort were closed for plumbing repairs, and I really needed to go. I attempted to call down to the visitor center to get permission to leave the room to use the bathrooms there. No one could find Dan Weekly, so I took it upon myself to walk the two hundred yards to the visitor center and use the bathroom. I was in uniform, as we were required to be, and as I approached the building a visitor stopped and asked me, "Where are the restrooms?" I gestured toward the large, glass doors of the visitor center and informed the gentleman that I was heading in that direction and he could follow me. As we approached the restroom the visitor engaged me in general friendly conversation. When I came back out into the hallway, much relieved, Dan Weekly was standing there, red-faced, glaring at me. "Who authorized you to talk to that visitor?," he blared at me, in his attempt at a deep, bullying voice.

"He only wanted to know where the restroom was," was my reply.

"I don't care what he asked you," Dan Weekly said I did not give you permission to talk to anyone. Now get your ass back up to the training room and I want a written note from you at the end of work today about what you missed during this little excursion."

I found out later that the superintendent had been around the corner listening to this exchange and appeared impressed that Dan was not taking any grief from one of the new employees. I was also later told that each day, Dan was submitting a written report on the progress of the new employees and that in his estimation we were not fit to work for the park service, but given time he could whip us into shape. During the two and half weeks, he had spent a total of ten minutes with us.

At the end of the work day I submitted the written summary as requested by Dan. I put a piece of paper on his desk that contained one word, "Nothing." The next morning, as I started up the walk to what had become our cell, Dan stopped me, and I prepared for another tirade. He said that he did not get my written note that he asked for. I told him I had put it on his desk, and we then went to his office to look for it. My note was sitting there. I picked it up, handed it to him, and walked out. He never brought it up again, but I think that act of defiance put me on his black list.

Later that same day Dan went home sick. The more experienced seasonal rangers broke us out of our room, divided us up into groups, and took us around the fort, showing us how to conduct guided tours. They made us swear not to tell Dan they had done this. It was the first real training we had received in three weeks. I started to have hope, and this gesture saved my interest in working for the National Park Service.

The next day the chief ranger came to our room and asked if anyone was interested in doing living history. Most of the group had no idea what this meant, but having visited other historic sites, and figuring it might get me out of this room, I quickly volunteered. One other seasonal and I were whisked away and taken under the chief ranger's wing and taught how to conduct programs dressed as the War of 1812 soldiers stationed at the fort. (I eventually developed a program where visitors entering the guard house of the fort would be recruited for the 1812 period army. That first summer I signed up over 6,000 volunteers.) The rest of the new employees were finally liberated by the end of that week to take up duties in the park.

We believed that the chief ranger had had enough and ordered them released. Dan Weekly took all the credit for training such an outstanding group of employees and made sure that everyone knew he was watching them.

At the end of the summer the decision was made to keep four additional seaonals on part-time for the winter. I was lucky enough to be selected to work three days a week. I jumped at the opportunity to keep working for the park service. However, I would have to work more directly under Dan Weekly. Several incidents occurred that eventually led to a downfall.

Dan had a large folder full of complimentary letters from visitors thanking him for his service to them. We all became suspicious when we noted that they all referred to him as Supervisory Park Technician Dan Weekly, when most people saw us as park rangers. All of these letters were from senior citizens like Dan. He was finally observed by one of my fellow employees, cornering some folks and giving them a business card, begging them to write a letter so he could keep his job. He told a story about how they were trying to force him to retire and replace him with a younger person. This story played well to older folks sympathizing with his plight and wanting to help. So he got lots of letters that looked impressive. This is what kept him in business with the superintendent because no one else was getting as many complimentary letters as Dan did.

One Saturday when it was just Dan, Martha, and myself working, a lightbulb went out in the recessed light fixture outside the restrooms. Dan decided to make this a training moment. He had me get a stepladder from downstairs and called Martha down from the fort. He had us one at a time climb the ladder and unscrew the bulb and then put the burned-out bulb back. We each had to do this three times while visitors came in and out of the visitor center with no one manning the front desk. Only once he was satisfied that we had the proper techniques down did he actually then let us do it several times more with a live bulb. This whole session took almost an hour when we could have had the maintenance guy on duty do it in three minutes. I like to think I could have figured this out myself, given five minutes. I heard Dan the next week bragging to the superintendent how he had made use of a slow weekend to conduct some cross training in other disciplines to his employees.

On another slow day Dan asked me to hand copy into a date book a list of schools that requested programs. There were a couple hundred schools listed. It took me the better part of the day in between working the front desk. Late that afternoon when Dan came by, I indicated the book and that I had finished. He became upset and challenged that I could not have done what he requested in that time. He accused me of not doing it properly or of cheating somehow. Dan had planned on this taking me several days to accomplish. Once he could find no fault with my work, the problem then became finding some other assignment to give me.

Several weeks later it was a very cold, windy, and rainy day. There were no visitors coming through the park, and the school groups we had scheduled for the day cancelled due to icy roads. One of the services we provided at Fort McHenry was to fly flags for individuals at the site where the "Star Spangled Banner" flag had flown. The flags would be returned to the owners after being unfurled for several minutes on the flagpole in the fort with a certificate testifying to this fact. These flags that were sent to the park had been building up in Dan's office, so he picked this cold, blustery day for my coworker Darschell and I to run twenty-plus flags up the pole. Although we did not think this was the best day to do this, we also knew it would be useless to argue with Dan. So with each of us carrying our armful of flag boxes, we pushed our way through the ice-laden wind to the fort.

Once there, we had to break the ice off the flagpole line in order to lower the flag we had up and to start raising all the flags we were given. Each flag was run up the pole and left flapping in the icy wind for a few minutes and then lowered back down. A new flag would be raised, and Darschell and I would neatly fold the previously raised wet flag into a perfect, proper triangle and place it respectfully back in its box. We stood exposed in the harsh weather until our hands were numb, and we took a break and tried to warm up in the guard room. Once feeling returned to our fingers, we again stepped out into the elements and continued to run up the flags. It took what seemed like forever to get this done. When we were finally finished, we packed everything up and marched our battered bodies back to the visitor center.

Inside the door stood Dan Weekly, waiting for us. "I watched the flagpole through the binoculars and I know you just raised the same flag up and down the whole time. Now I want you both to go back up there and do it right."

Darschell, who was a very thin, African American woman, stood there trembling from the cold. We were both soaked through. She glared at Dan with a look that would have killed most men and said, "We flew every one of these flags and you can look through them yourself and see they are wet because you sent us up there on such a sorry day. If you want them flown again, you can drag your sorry ass up there and do it yourself." She then stomped off.

I told Dan that what she had said was true, and just because he would have put the same flag up and down the pole does not mean that we would have done the same. And then I stomped off.

Eventually, the wet flags were sent off to the owners just as Darschell and I had packed them that day.

In February we had one of those weekends when the temperatures soured into the sixties. This followed several weeks of drab and cold winter weather. Everyone in the Baltimore area came out of their homes to stretch and celebrate a beautiful day. Thousands swarmed to the open spaces of Fort McHenry. Working that day were Darschell, John, and myself, supervised by Dan Weekly. People were literally climbing the walls of the fort. Several local ruffians had shown up and were throwing rocks at the buildings. John and I were in the fort and trying to catch up to these kids, communicating with the park's antiquated seven-pound portable radios. Darschell called from the visitor center for one of us to get to the phone. She informed

John that Dan, upon hearing us on the radio, had said, "They must think they are Starsky and Hutch. They'll pay for this." Dan had then gone back into the basement. Darschell was overwhelmed with visitors and followed Dan in an attempt get some help. She found him passed out on the lunchroom table. Dan would not respond to Darschell's attempts to awake him. Upon hearing this story, John headed toward the visitor center. As he approached the building he saw Dan Weekly walk through the parking lot, get in his car, and drive off. When John asked Darschell what had happened she knew nothing, and Dan had not told her he was leaving. He did not return the rest of the day and left the three of us to fend for ourselves.

Dan called in sick the next few days and nothing was ever said to us about what had happened to him. When I got my written performance review from Dan, he noted that I used the radio too much and could not stand up under pressure. I remember the resentment I felt and the utter defeat, knowing that my career chances were most likely gone with this on my record. I went to Tom Westmoreland, the chief ranger, and he told me not to worry and that he would take care of it. The next day I got a new evaluation that was glowing and signed by the chief ranger. Dan's signature was nowhere in sight.

Dan continued to bungle along, and two people quit, not being able to stand him any longer. My strong desire to be a park ranger and the dedication of my fellow employees were all that kept my faith in this career decision. But tension between Dan and I continued to build after the chief ranger changed my evaluation. We refused to call him chief, as I argued that he was not the chief ranger. Every time I called him Dan, his face would turn red and then purple. Other employees stopped calling him chief, and he seethed.

This all came to a head one very crowded spring day in the visitor center. Springtime is busy at Fort McHenry, with school and tour groups lining the parking lot with busses. On this day I had a scheduled two-bus school group show up a half-hour late for their program, which included the introductory film in the visitor center followed by a guided tour of the fort. As the teachers came into the visitor center, I also had an unscheduled tour leader come to the information desk. The tour was a busload of forty retired folks who had just driven in from Washington, D.C. Knowing from experience that most retired groups that came to the park had a first priority of using the restrooms, I arranged for the eighty school children to move directly into the theater for the fifteen-minute film. While that was going on, the seniors could use the bathrooms, check out the exhibits, and visit the gift shop. Once the students were done, they could be ushered to the fort for their tour, and the seniors could then enjoy the film. Both group leaders were happy with this arrangement, and I was quite proud of my organizational skills. From out of nowhere entered Dan Weekly. He looked around the crowed visitor center and bellowed to me, "What is going on here?" I ran down my plan for him, and he immediately told me I did not know what I was doing. The senior citizens should have first priority for the movie, and we could get the kids in there at the same time. I told him again that it was already worked out, but he would not hear of it. He ordered me to put all the groups into the theater. I told him, in what I have to admit was an insolent tone, "They will all be crammed in there like sardines, but if you are so good at this, you put them all in the theater." So he did. I was then ordered to do the introduction for the film, which came before each program.

Even though my nose was a bit out of joint from Dan's treatment, I went to the front of the theater and looked out across the crowd. In the back were forty senior citizens crammed into plastic seats. Many were squirming due to being packed in so tight, and I am sure they were dreaming about using a bathroom. The middle school students were packed into the rest of the chairs, with about thirty or so of them sitting on the floor. Their teachers were standing, lining the brick wall to my right. I welcomed these sardines to the park and gave the basic orientation information and pushed the button on the wall to start the projector. When I left the theater and walked down the exit ramp, Dan Weekly was waiting for me.

He spoke to me in a surprisingly fatherly tone and said,

"Now that was a fine introduction talk you gave, but you are supposed to stand on the stage when you give it, not the floor." I could tell he was proud that he had taken over and worked all this out, but he still had to correct me for something.

I had had about enough and responded, "Well Dan, I am six foot four, and I feel too high leering over everyone when I stand on the stage so I stand on the floor."

"I don't care where you feel comfortable. It is policy that you stand on the stage."

At that point I blew my youthful and impatient temper, blasting back at him, "Well, if it is policy that means it is written down. I have never seen it written down that I have to stand on the stage."

"Well, I am your boss and if I tell you it's policy, then it's policy."

"It's not policy if it's not written down. You don't even know, do you?"

At that point I do not remember Dan's exact words, because there were so many colorful ones, but the crux of what he said was, "You're fired."

"I'm fired? You're firing me?"

"Yes now get your ass out of this park and never come back."

We must have gotten a bit loud, because as I walked back toward the rear door of the visitor center to leave, the chief ranger met me and asked what was going on. I informed him that Dan had just fired me and that I was leaving. He told me to hold on, that Dan had no authority to fire me, and to give him a few minutes. The superintendent was gone that day, and the chief ranger asked me to take a seat in that office. After closing the door he went looking for Dan. I could hear loud voices in the hallway, and then even louder voices in the chief ranger's office. The next thing I knew, with a slam of the door, I looked out the window and saw Dan Weekly stomping out into the parking lot, getting in his car, and driving off. The chief ranger came in and told me I was not fired and to get back to the front desk. That was all he said, so I figured I must have been re-hired, and I went back to work.

Dan did not show up to work for two weeks. No one had heard from him, and the chief ranger and superintendent kept calling his telephone. They even went by his home but did not find him. The third week, his daughter called to let the park know that Dan had been checked into the Veterans' Hospital for treatment. Dan had been in the hospital since the day after our confrontation, but his daughter would not give out any information as to his illness. The chief ranger finally went to the hospital to visit Dan and found that he was isolated in the mental ward, following a breakdown. They had also found that he was addicted to prescription painkillers and that he was suffering from withdrawal. Dan was never to return to work for the National Park Service.

Dan did, however, return to the park several months later, accompanied by a representative of the Federal Employees' Union, who requested a meeting with the superintendent to file grievances against the park. It quickly became apparent during this meeting that Dan had not fully recovered from his mental breakdown, and he made numerous outlandish accusations, mainly against those employees who worked under him, for conspiring to drive him nuts. About halfway through Dan's presentation of complaints, the union representative had to explain to him that he could not file a grievance against employees that were under him, and the representative apologized and excused himself from the proceedings. Dan finally left, still shouting threats as he walked through the parking lot.

A few days later his daughter again called the park, this time requesting information for her father on applying for a disability retirement. Dan had been readmitted to the veteran's hospital, where he remained for an extended period. By the time Dan was released from treatment, I had obtained a permanent job with the park service, gotten married, and transferred to another park.

Although these experiences were difficult ones to deal with

while I was attempting to start my career, I was able to learn quite a bit from them. The confidence and support shown by my fellow park rangers and Chief Ranger Tom Westmoreland fortified my desire to make the National Park Service my way of life. I also learned a lot from Dan Weekly on how not to be a supervisor. Although Dan may have been a much more affective supervisor when he was in the navy and was not dealing with a dependency on prescription painkillers, in his park service career he only showed me how not to deal with people. Many times in my own career as a supervisor and manager, I have looked back at my experiences with Dan Weekly and realized how he had inadvertently directed me on how not to handle a situation. We can learn from all our experiences, whether they are positive or negative. At times, this is a hard lesson to learn and remember.

The World of the Supernatural

Many people remember some instance in their lives when they lay awake at night, unable to fall asleep, due to a story they had heard around a campfire or perhaps from staying up too late to watch a scary movie on TV. The National Park Service manages many sites that were important in the history of our country, and those sites are rich in a wide variety of such stories. It would be impossible to be exposed to this much history without running into unexplained happenings. Now, the reader should not infer that I believe in ghosts, but what happened to me could leave you wondering. I have to admit, it does make me wonder. All I can say is that what you read here is based on my experiences, as best my memory serves me.

Early in my career, I was stationed at Fort McHenry National Monument and Historic Shrine in Baltimore, Maryland. Another area also under the administration of the superintendent at Fort McHenry was Hampton House National Historic Site, located just north of Baltimore in Towson, Maryland. Hampton House was a mansion built by the Ridgely family during the 1780s and today serves as one of our country's finest examples of Georgian architecture. The house is constructed of brick that was produced by slaves on the property and then covered with stucco in a faded pink color. At the time the house was built, it was one of the largest homes in America and the Ridgelys were one of our young country's wealthiest families, having made their fortune from the shipping industry and iron ore. The house remained in the Ridgely family's ownership until the 1940s, when it was donated to the National Park Service.

In the 1970s, Hampton House was a National Park Service area but was managed under a formal agreement by the Maryland Society for the Preservation of Antiquities. This was a private historical foundation which had their main offices in the basement of the mansion itself. As a result of this arrangement there were no park service personnel assigned to the site, and it was the responsibility of the staff at Fort McHenry to keep track of the site's activities from a distance.

Hampton House. Photo Courtesy of the National Park Service

One of my duties was to investigate on behalf of the National Park Service any incidents or problems that occurred at Hampton House. This duty typically involved receiving a phone call at Fort McHenry, driving for move than an hour to Towson, and interviewing the people that made the initial report. Needless to say, this was not an idyllic situation. Some days I would have to investigate minor thefts and vandalism, and in some instances there were reports of supernatural activities and ghosts.

Hampton House was well known throughout the area as "haunted," and there was even a book published retelling ghost stories that were reputed to have occurred there over the last two hundred years. What made the reports of several incidents that occurred while I worked in Baltimore interesting and credible was that they were reported by all kinds of people, people from different parts of the world. Most of these individuals had no ideas about or any prior knowledge of any ghost stories at Hampton House.

On one such trip, I investigated reports of a thin, strangely dressed man who had been seen in the formal gardens behind the house itself. The man was seen wearing a stovepipe hat and a short coat with tails. Numerous people had reported seeing this man while they were visiting the site during a two-week period, and they had thought that he was a historically costumed employee. But when they would attempt to approach him to ask questions, he would turn away and simply walk into the woods. No one ever saw him again, once he had reached this part of the grounds. One of the guides from the house even took photos of the man from a distance. When the photo prints were returned, they showed a beautiful picture of the gardens, but no man.

In another instance, a group was meeting in a conference room located in the basement of the house when they were disturbed by a tapping on the floor of the room above them. The occupants described the sound as that of the tapping of a cane on the wood floor. Finally, the noise so distracted the group to the point that no work was being accomplished. One participant was sent upstairs to request that whoever was making the racket to please stop it. As the chosen person started up the stairs, the participant met another person coming down, who was sent to ask the basement group to stop tapping on the basement ceiling. Upon looking into this happening, I noted that the ceiling in the basement was made up of the floorboards of the room above. There was no space in between, and you could look up through the floor cracks into the room above. There were no pipes or heating ducts nor any other source that I could determine that could have made this noise, which had been so disturbing to more than twenty people, both above and below this floor.

There were large, interior wooden shutters in all the windows and doors on the first floor of the house. This type of shutter was referred to as "Indian Shutters," designed so they could be closed from the inside to aid in the defense of the structure if under any hostile attack. All the shutters at Hampton House had a wooden slat that was placed across them and into grooves when the shutters were closed to prevent their being pushed open from the outside. To add to modern-day security, the park service had installed an electronic alarm system that included magnetic contacts on these shutters. This system was designed so that once all the shutters were closed and locked, the alarm was turned on. If any of the shutters were opened, the electric contact would be broken, and the alarm would then be activated.

A frequent occurrence that I had been told about involved the procedure in which the guides came to work in the morning, entered the house, opened the side door, and then turned off the alarm which had been engaged since the shutters' closing the evening before. When the guides made their rounds, what they found were the shutters in the library standing open, with the early morning sun streaming in. If the shutters had been opened during the night or if the alarm had been turned on with the shutters open, a siren would have sounded, and an alert would have been relayed to the local police department. The system was checked and found to be functioning properly, and no one had received an alarm signal. There was no explanation of why the alarm did not go off when the shutters were opened or how anyone could enter the house without setting off an alarm. After this had happened on several occasions, one of the blue-haired, older ladies who worked as a guide told me, "You know who really opens the shutters, don't you?" When I answered that I had absolutely no idea, she confidently stood erect on her toes and in an all-knowing manner informed me, "Why, it is Mr. Ridgely, of course, trying to get some light to read." Later, I went back and compared the times in which the shutters had been found open to a calendar and found that all these incidents had occurred within a few days of a full moon.

Now, I remained much the skeptic of all these doings at the time and did not fully believe that any of this was the result of anything other than overactive imaginations and the creaking and groaning of an old house. What I did not know was that my turn to experience these unknown powers would soon come about.

Plans had been made to have a needle point show at Hampton House in January 1977. This show was to include not only new pieces of art that were submitted in a competition but also a display of historic needlepoint containing some works of Martha Washington and several other early first ladies. These art pieces were to be exhibited in the rooms on the first and second floors, which were completely furnished in Ridgely possessions, most dating from the late 1700s and early 1800s. In order to hold the show, the insurance company covering the historic exhibition insisted on there being twenty-four-hour security on site.

There I was, sitting behind the information desk at Fort McHenry on a cold, wintry day, just praying for a visitor to come through the door so I would have someone to talk to, when the chief ranger called me to his office. It was then that I discovered that I had been volunteered, along with one other ranger, Courtney, to spend two weeks, twenty-four hours a day, at Hampton House, protecting needlework. Arrangements were being made to supply us with food and other necessities, and we were to remain in the house or on the immediate grounds during this entire period. Being a rather new employee, and always wanting to make a good impression, I was enthused about this assignment. Later, it dawned on me that we were talking about two whole weeks sitting in an old house. Oh well, duty was duty, and it had called.

Courtney and I moved into one of the bedrooms on the third floor of the house and set up camp. This level of the house had not been restored and consisted of a long hallway running the length of the house, with a dozen or more rooms off of either side. These rooms had originally been used as bedrooms for younger family members and guests. When we arrived, each was a dust-filled room with louver-slatted wooden doors that opened into the main hallway. The room next to ours had a row of wooden pegs on the wall that was shared with our room. On these pegs were hung dozens of horse harnesses that had been used by the Ridgelys for their racehorses during the 1800s. Other than these harnesses, the other rooms were relatively empty. The main stairs came up at the end of the hallway near our room. In the middle of this floor was a spiral stairway that led up to the large cupola (a sort of ornate observation tower), one of Hampton House's distinctive architectural features, which was in the center of its slate roof. This was the top floor of the house, and there were no other living or storage areas above us. We spread our sleeping bags on the bedroom's floor and prepared for our stay.

I was more than aware of the many ghost stories and strange happenings that were connected with Hampton House. Although at the time I was a strong skeptic of these "tall tales," I would be lying to say that this bountiful knowledge had not come to surface the first few nights that we slept in the house. As in any old houses, there were a number of strange noises in the night. This was January, and the area was experiencing record-breaking cold temperatures. All over Baltimore, water mains were freezing underground and bursting, spewing fountains of water into the air and freezing ice on every surface. At Hampton House the wind literally howled at night through the hand-blown glass windows, and the old furnace and heating pipes that dated back to the 1920s were working overtime. The hot water running through the heating pipes sounded at times like a mass of blacksmiths hammering on anvils. Any imagination could mistake these sounds for an army of ghosts, marching up and down the halls. After two nights of disturbed sleep, I became accustomed to the normal noises of the house, got my imagination under control, and was able to sleep like a rock.

Our stay had gone without incident. We were becoming a bit bored watching needlepoint all day and spent more and more time just wandering through the house at night. On the Monday morning of our second week, Courtney was awakened just before dawn by what he thought was a sound in the hallway outside our door. He slowly got to his feet and looked toward the sound and saw what he thought was a shadow or silhouette through the slats of the louvered door. As he approached the door, the shadow appeared to move down the hall, away from the stairs. I awoke as Courtney neared the door. He threw it open, jumping into the hall to find nothing. Courtney was very animated as he relayed to me what had happened, and I accused him of pulling my leg. We both got up and searched through the entire house, finding nothing. I classified this entire episode as Courtney's overactive imagination or his just trying to get my goat.

The Society for the Preservation of Antiquities had a curator who was assigned to Hampton House, and his office was on the second floor in the only room that was not open to the public. He informed us that he would be working late in his office that night, and that there was a cot in the backroom where he would most likely spend the night if his work took him beyond eleven o'clock. We checked the alarm system and the house thoroughly before midnight (Courtney had insisted on spending more time checking everything out) and stopped by to say goodnight to the curator, who was pouring over some original letters written by members of the Ridgely family. He said that he did not realize how late it was, and that he was going to stay and turn in. We then went to our campsite on the third

floor to get some sleep ourselves. We had just started to wan-
der off into dreamland when we heard the curator yelling for
us downstairs. Courtney and I quickly ran to his room, which
still had the door closed and locked from the inside. The curator fumbled about and finally unlocked the door for us, and we
entered his work area. The curator told us that he had left his
work on the table and had gone to the backroom to lie down.
Shortly thereafter, he could hear the papers on his desk rustling
like someone was going through them. He remembered thinking that perhaps it was mouse on his desk. Then it sounded
like someone had taken their hand and shoved everything onto
the floor and had then walked out of the room, opening and
then closing the door leading into the hallway. The curator had
jumped up and ran into the room, finding everything as he had
left it and the door still locked from the inside. It was at this
point that he had called for us. He insisted that he had still been
wide awake and had not even started to doze off when this all
had happened. Once again, I remained skeptical of this story,
but I did note for my own reference that the curator then very
sheepishly left, getting into his car and going to his home for
the rest of the night.

On Wednesday, after closing for the day, Courtney and I
spent from six o'clock in the evening until after midnight searching the interior of the house. There had been so many architectural studies and rehabilitation projects done on the house that
we knew there were no secret passages or rooms. We searched
so thoroughly that we even included the inside of the furnace,
under desks, in closets, window seats, and wardrobes. In other
words, every crevice and crack we could find. We tested the
alarm system several times and found that it was functioning
properly. We finally returned to our room on the third floor a
little after midnight.

We had just lain down to attempt to sleep when I heard what
sounded like footsteps entering the room next to ours. I could
distinctly hear the boards creaking and the sound move across
the room. Then there was a sound as if someone had taken their

hand and run it down the wall of horse harnesses causing them to swing on the pegs. This was followed by footsteps exiting the room and moving down the hall, away from the stairway and toward the empty rooms. I laid there for what seemed an eternity, wondering if I had really heard these sounds, when I rolled over to look at Courtney and found him lying on his back with his eyes as big as saucers. I asked if he had just heard something and he quickly replied, "Damn straight." Dressed only in our long johns, we both jumped out of our sleeping bags, grabbed our handguns, and ran to the next room, looking a bit like ghosts ourselves. What we found were several of the harnesses still swaying slowly on the pegs.

We made a hasty search of the third floor rooms. Finding nothing, we returned to put on our uniforms. We commenced a detailed search of the entire house from top to bottom, finding nothing out of place. On the first floor we paid special attention, checking the alarm contacts and all the bars on the interior windows and door shutters. The great hall in the center of the house had iron bars that went across the interior of the doors, and all these were in place. During this process, neither Courtney nor I left each other's sight. We again ran an alarm check with the security company that monitored the system and found that everything was still functioning.

We then returned to the great hall, where there was a telephone at the main desk. I had told my father that I would call him if anything strange happened during my stay, and I decided that this was the time. I was sitting at the desk with my father on the line, and Courtney was standing in front of me shining his flashlight around the room, when I heard a gasp. I looked in the direction of his light and saw that the iron bar across one of the doors had been removed and placed in the corner by the door. I felt my throat constrict and my stomach turn as I looked toward the door. We had both checked this bar not ten minutes before, and it was in place, securing the door, at that time. I know we both remembered immediately that one of the old Ridgely family ghost stories involved several children coming down the main stairs in the middle of the night and seeing this same bar float through the air and land exactly where we were looking at it now.

Our evening had not quite ended yet. There was a large grandfather clock that sat in the great hall, having been imported from England by the Ridgelys in the early 1800s. I had been told early in our stay that this clock had not worked in over one hundred years. Suddenly, this same clock now started to chime.

I am not sure what emotions were running through our minds at this point, but I do know that the next thing I remembered was the both of us sitting outside in the park service's pick-up truck. And that is exactly where we spent the rest of the night.

The next evening, after everything had closed down (but before dark), I went up to the cupola at the very top of the house and for some reason just started talking to the air saying, "Look, we are here to protect your house from being damaged or vandalized. We are only going to be here for a few days, and then we will be gone." At this point Courtney came up from below me and asked what I was doing. I replied, "Nothing." And he said, "Well it sounds good. Keep it up."

To this day I cannot give an explanation of what happened on those few winter nights, and I do not really try to understand it. I do know that after I had that little talk in the cupola, nothing else unusual happened during the rest of our stay. I assure you that if another incident had occurred, I would have known about it. This was because I spent the majority of the rest of our time in that house wide awake.

Living in a National Park

Some park areas offer housing to employees within the park. The intent is to benefit the government by having the people who live in the houses maintain them and to be on site to provide emergency response for the protection of visitors and resources. Having people living in the park can also serve as a deterrent to criminal activity. For many positions, it is required that the employee live in park housing. In other cases, the park area is so remote or surrounded by government-protected lands that there are no options for private housing available.

There is a misconception shared by much of the public that employees get to live for free in these houses, with beautiful views of mountain streams and landscapes. The fantasy includes a beautiful log cabin nestled in a pine forest, high in the mountains. The reality is, the houses we lived in were of cheap construction, not well insulated, and had views of paved and chain-link-fenced maintenance areas. Several, were what are referred to as "Mission 66" houses, the result of the last large investment our government made in the national parks in the late 1950s and 1960s. These houses, found in parks throughout the country, have the same basic floor plan. The two we lived in on the Blue Ridge Parkway were built on concrete slabs that promoted dampness and mold, our health suffered, and many of our personal items suffered mold damage.

Once I applied for a job at Shenandoah National Park. My

wife and I made a visit to introduce ourselves and to find out more about the position. My hopes were dashed when the supervisor took us to view the required housing that went with the job. It consisted of an apartment of about 400 square feet that was part of a row of such apartments built of cinder block on a concrete slab. The kitchenette had a half-size sink, a miniature stove, and a bar-size refrigerator. The bathroom was so small that if I were sitting on the toilet my legs would be in the shower. When examining the green-painted cinder block walls, we noticed that in several places where there should have been mortar, you could see through to the outside. Then the supervisor topped this off by telling us that they had hoped to hire a single person, who could share the apartment with a seasonal employee in the summer! Needless to say, on the way home, my wife convinced me to withdraw my application.

Rents are charged for employee housing, and are based on what is being paid in the local area. Many parks are located in resort areas, which drives up the rental costs. At one point the rent for the housing that park rangers were required to live in at the Statue of Liberty in Liberty Park was based on the Manhattan rents in New York City. That rent worked out to be more than the park rangers were paid. It took a special act of congress to give these employees a break in their rent. When my wife and I were finally able to purchase our own home, our mortgage payments turned out to be less than what we were paying in rent to the National Park Service.

During my park service career, I worked for several supervisors who had lived in park housing for their entire careers. Once retirement came, they had to move out, with no home to go to and no equity built up with which to purchase a house. One such supervisor and his wife could not even agree on what town or what part of the country to move to.

There are many other horror stories about employees living in rat-infested, ancient mobile homes. One such mobile home that was used to house permanent park rangers was converted to seasonal dormitories. It was known as the mouse house, and each year there was a competition to see which resident could catch the most mice in an impressive number of traps set out daily throughout the mobile home.

Living in park housing, you are also subject to being called out after-hours and are caught answering visitor questions when they phone you or knock on your door. When working on the Blue Ridge Parkway in North Carolina, I managed an area that required a written permit for backcountry camping. My wife, who was not a park employee, issued more permits from our house than any of the park offices. There is generally not much privacy in a park residence. When living in the Fredericksburg and Spotsylvania National Military Park, I once had a visitor walk into our house, demanding a tour. I called out to him from the bathtub I had just entered, informing him that this was a private residence. He informed me that he was a taxpayer and that this was a government building, so he had a right to look around. I got out of the tub, wrapped a towel around my waist, and literally chased him out of the house. We were much more careful about keeping the doors locked after that.

One day I was at home eating lunch when there was a knock at the door. I opened it to find a short, grizzled old man with three days of white beard and a twinkle in his eye. He was wearing an old, beat-up fedora hat, a gingham button-up shirt, and worn denim overalls. He said, "I just wanted to warn you, if you got kids, that there are rattlesnakes around here."

I was well aware of that fact and responded, "Well, thanks for letting me know about that. Did you see a snake?"

"Yeah, I just killed a big one on the road right behind your house."

This took me by surprise, since a major part of my job was to protect wildlife in the park. I asked him if he had run over it with his truck. "No," he said. "I kilt it with a tire iron."

"A tire iron?" was the only response I could muster, with even more surprise. He then took me out to his truck and proudly displayed a two-foot-long, angled tire iron. I gave him a brief lecture, explaining how all the wildlife in the park is protected, including poisonous snakes. The little man just looked at me like I was crazy. I could not bring myself to charge him for any violation, and I let him go with my ill-received warning.

After finishing my lunch, I went out to the road's shoulder to see if I could find the dead snake. What I found was one of the largest rattlesnakes I had ever seen. It was almost five-feet long and was so large in the middle that I could not touch my thumb to my fingers around it. I could not imagine that little old man doing battle with this huge monster, armed only with his little tire iron. He must have really hated rattlesnakes.

You never knew what visitors would want next. One time our telephone rang at two-thirty in the morning, and I got up groggily to answer it. I babbled, "Hello, this is the Blue Ridge Parkway," expecting to hear a report of another emergency.

A perky woman's voice responded, "Oh hi, I am coming up there for a picnic later today, and I wanted to know what the weather forecast was."

I was incredulous at being awakened from a deep sleep to answer such a question. But I tried to be professional and responded to her,. "Well, according to the news at eleven o'clock…"

She cut me off, "No, no, I want the latest forecast."

I replied, "That is the latest forecast I have. You could call the U.S. Weather Service for more information."

"Are you being smart with me?" the woman said. "I called you for the information, and I don't want you passing me on to some other bureaucrat."

"This is a residence, not a twenty-four-hour office, and you just got me out of bed."

"You are a government employee and I pay your salary. I don't like your attitude and I have a mind to write my Congressman to complain."

"That is your right if you want, but I do not have any other weather information," I told her. At that point she hung up on me. Several days later, I was ordered to produce a written apology to the woman in response to a congressional complaint.

Another middle-of-the-night call came from a man who wanted to let me know that his pregnant wife was due any day.

The man was planning to go trout fishing that morning on a remote stream that was not even within the park, and he wanted to give my phone number to his wife. She could call me before going to the hospital, and I would then track him down to let him know she had gone. I informed him I could not provide this service, and the man became irate. Once again, another written complaint was sent to the park superintendent.

So the moral of these few examples is that living in a national park is not the ideal situation that most people envision. You end up living with your job twenty-four-hours a day. Most times, your neighbors are the same people you work with every day. For young park rangers just starting on their career, this can be a positive experience, as long as everyone gets along. For a family, it can be challenging and a bit confining. There is no ability to just relax and not answer the telephone or radio because you are tired or are spending time with your kids, or having a fight with your spouse. Your fellow employees know if you are home, and you cannot get away with much. I would compare it to the old cliché of living in a fish bowl. It can be frustrating at times. I remember a friend of mine whose park residence was just within the entrance to a large and very busy campground in the Great Smokey Mountains National Park. The campground was typical of most park service areas, in that the facilities were limited and did not include showers. People were constantly coming to his house and demanding that his wife let them in so they could take a shower. His half-joking proposed solution was to someday get a large German shepherd and to train it to attack people who were wearing cameras around their necks.

When the day finally came that my wife and I were able to buy our own home outside the park, we were thrilled. I was a bit concerned, as a fairly new supervisor who had lived at his work place for ten years, that this would be a hard adjustment. After all, I had been at the center of the action for all of that time. The first night I drove home to my own house, it took less than thirty seconds to get over that concern.

Law Enforcement versus Management in the National Park Service

An issue of contention that kept raising its head during my ranger career centered on management of law enforcement duties of park rangers in our national parks. The original act of congress that established the National Park Service charged the agency with providing protection for the natural and cultural resources and the people in our parks. The National Park Service was further empowered under federal legislation to designate employees that meet specified requirements of training, fitness, and security background clearances as commissioned federal law enforcement officers. These employees have the authority to enforce federal and state laws within areas that are under the management of the National Park Service. These rangers can make arrests, conduct investigations, execute warrants, and function in the full capacity of any other federal law enforcement officer.

When the first national park was established at Yellowstone, the U.S. Army was tasked with protecting the park's resources and visitors. Within a few years, it was determined that a civilian force of rangers or wardens was needed to fulfill this responsibility. Those first hired rangers were rough and tough wilderness men, given the job of protecting wildlife and people. They were heavily armed and had many hair-rising adventures working alone in the wild.

It is surprising to many people to learn that most national park managers and superintendents have never worked as a park ranger with law enforcement responsibilities. The park service is an agency with law enforcement officers managed and supervised by non-law enforcement personnel. In fact, many of these managers tend to exhibit a negative mindset about law enforcement in their attitudes and decision making. I have to say that most park superintendents that I worked under did not want anything to do with law enforcement responsibilities or the employees with those duties. These superintendents had trouble trusting the employees who had graduated from training at the Federal Law Enforcement Training Center, who in many cases had years of experience in the field dealing with the public in its darkest aspects. Park rangers are the employees that have to step into harm's way when people or resources are threatened. This missing piece of managerial experience has contributed to a lack of understanding and a fear of the responsibility and professional procedures of law enforcement. Many managers had difficulty relinquishing direct control of any function of their operations because they did not inherently trust others to bear this responsibility. These were factors that contributed to park superintendents improperly managing law enforcement operations. This created, in many cases, friction between managers and field park rangers who were dedicated to doing their jobs.

I once attended a supervisors' meeting in a large park where the superintendent was angry because a friend of his had received a speeding ticket from one of the rangers. The ranger was ordered to void the ticket, an order which he justifiably refused to comply with. The superintendent then got up before the group and stated that he would prefer to get rid of every park ranger in the park because he could run a better operation with just maintenance personnel. Of course, these comments did not make the rangers in the crowd feel valued or in turn supportive of their boss. Following the meeting, all radar units in the park were removed from the field "for repair" and were not returned. This was the manager's solution for punishing the rangers and for reducing complaints about law enforcement actions.

The next spring, the budget to the Protection Division in this same park was greatly reduced. Law enforcement rangers were required to spend the majority of their time collecting fees in the campgrounds due to the lack of seasonal employees that normally performed this task. By late summer, officials in the regional office noted a sharp increase in the number of serious motor vehicle accidents and more than a doubling of visitor deaths since the previous year, with the number of people killed within the park approaching thirty. This resulted in a high level of concern with why so many people were being killed in this park. Immediately, the blame was placed on the field rangers and supervisors for not doing their jobs. The money appeared seemingly from nowhere for each ranger to work a required two hours of overtime every day to conduct traffic enforcement, and the missing radar units were returned to the rangers. As a result, the number of accidents and fatalities significantly decreased during the heaviest traffic months in the fall.

I tell this story to illustrate the frustration faced by law enforcement commissioned rangers working for managers who have no understanding of the importance of their role in resource and visitor safety. The manager from the above story continued to project his negative attitude toward his staff until a tragedy changed that park forever. It unfortunately took a park ranger 's death, being shot and killed in the line of duty, for the manager to realize that the enforcement of laws and regulations is not merely an inconvenience or a game.

This lack of understanding has also contributed to problems of the agency's perceptions of what role the park rangers have and how they should function. This is exemplified in the issue of whether or not rangers should wear firearms.

In the early 1970s, many park managers were quite liberal minded and came from non-law enforcement or park protection backgrounds. The first superintendents I worked for came from maintenance and administrative backgrounds. They were proficient at meeting bureaucratic requirements and keeping up maintenance of facilities but had weaknesses in other areas. These superintendents were emphatic about the public not seeing rangers wearing guns. They felt this presented an overbearing and negative image to the visitors. Rangers were still expected to deal with any difficult people or crimes that were committed in the parks, but they were not permitted to be readily equipped to safely handle such incidents.

One superintendent at a large park located in the center of a major city would not permit his rangers to wear guns. After several incidents occurred when employees were placed in danger, the superintendent relented and allowed only supervisory rangers in the protection division to carry concealed weapons during the day. This park received a visit from a head of a foreign power, and the U.S. Secret Service requested fifty additional rangers for security. Rangers were called in from all over the region to boost the park's staff for this event. Once they arrived, the superintendent addressed the group and told them to take off their guns and their defensive equipment. He did not want them to be seen armed in public. The secret service stepped in and tried to overrule this order. The superintendent threw a fit, causing a huge scene. The rangers ended up being assigned duties more as ushers and doormen, and the secret service brought in other agencies to assist them with their security needs.

Two years later, a man walked into this same park's visitor center and demanded a permit to conduct a public demonstration as guaranteed under the First Amendment. He stated that he was the head of an American Nazi group that wanted to conduct an anti-Jewish and Israel march. Due to the protections of the U.S. Constitution, the park could not deny the permit. They could only place conditions to limit and locate the specific activities within the park. This city's Jewish population was outraged that such a permit would be issued, and the media and local politicians echoed this anger. The news media further churned the mix, resulting in park employees and specifically the superintendent receiving death threats in the form of telephone calls, letters, and telegrams. The National Park Service and the FBI scrambled to track down the threat sources and to learn more about the group that was planning the demonstration.

Almost immediately, rangers were detailed to the park from all over the region. I was one of those sent, having been given twelve hours to report for duty. This time, there was a great difference in the park's superintendent's reception: He was greatly appreciative of everyone's response, and he wanted every ranger armed to the teeth and providing twenty-four-hour security for he and his family. Surveillance was conducted on his home within the park, foot patrols of the area were increased around the clock, and rangers were placed in plain clothes to accompany the superintendent's family members to school, work, and even the opera.

One night, my partner and I were assigned to a foot patrol in the superintendent's neighborhood, and two other rangers were assigned in a surveillance position in a vacant apartment across from the superindent's home. We had been given information on a vehicle and a physical description of an individual who had been seen in the area a few days earlier. A tag check showed that the vehicle's owner had a record of being connected to a vocal and perhaps militant Jewish group. We were to keep our eyes especially sharp for this individual or his car.

It was pouring down rain that night, so the gutters were running full, flushing the daily urban debris around our feet. My partner and I had been walking around for the first three hours of our sixteen-hour shift and were already very wet and cold. We slipped into the surveillance apartment to warm up and dry off for a few minutes and had just stripped off all our rain-soaked gear when one of the rangers assigned to the inside duty called out, "Shit, it's him."

We all ran to the windows and saw the vehicle we were looking for slowly moving down the narrow, historic, brick-cobbled street. We scrambled to get our dripping gear back on. Before we could get out the backdoor, a call came over the radio: the vehicle was making a second pass in front of the house. We sprinted on the wet, brick sidewalk around to the front of the building only to discover that the vehicle was gone. It had driven by slowly twice in opposite directions. Backup was on the way. At this point the city police department had been told by the mayor not to get involved, so no help would come from them. That made any backup a bit farther away. One of the local rangers, who was going off-duty, pulled up in his personal vehicle. We told him what was going on, and he took off in an attempt to relocate the suspicious car and driver.

My partner and I walked to the end of the block to get around the two hundred-year-old row houses to check the rear of the superintendent's house. In the narrow cobblestone alley, we found the suspect's car parked, behind the house. We approached the vehicle with our guns drawn and found it was empty. There was no indication of where the driver had gone, and the car was locked.

Between the alley and the house was an ornate, wrought iron gate in a low brick wall that surrounded a small ancient and menacing-looking cemetery. Our backup units of rangers and U.S. Park Police were still trying to reach us. While my partner stayed by the car, I began a slow search of the cemetery with my gun drawn in front of me. The cemetery was full of three- to five-foot high tombstones and raised crypts. It provided excellent cover for someone trying to hide. The rain continued to poor down, almost blinding me and preventing my flashlight from penetrating the night. We were concerned that the driver of the car was using the cemetery to approach the rear of the superintendent's house with a bomb or maybe to break in.

Suddenly I heard the welcoming sound of tires squealing on the wet pavement, and two carloads of help arrived in the alley. I then took up a position where I had cover but could see the space between the back of the house and the cemetery wall, which was much lower at this point.

Within minutes my partner radioed to inform me that a bomb dog had given a positive response to the car. This meant that a bomb or bomb-making materials could be in the car. I hunkered down a bit lower behind my cover, which was the largest granite crypt I could find.

At that moment, a man was seen walking from the far end of the alley toward the group of officers surrounding the car. When challenged, his response was, "Hey, what's going on?" He was identified as the owner of the car and was placed in custody. The FBI showed up about this time, and the man was instantly whisked off to some other location. In the meantime, the officer with the bomb dog was able to verify that no bombs were in the car. Another dog was brought in, and they began a detailed search of the area. Homes were evacuated, and the search went on for hours.

In custody, the suspect's story was that he was visiting a friend who lived around the corner, and that he had spilled antifreeze on the back floorboard of the car earlier that day. The friend he was visiting turned out to be a young lady that he had been bothering for a date, and he was in the early stages of stalking her. The FBI decided to hold on to this guy for forty-eight hours. The car was towed. Lab tests later proved that indeed antifreeze was in the rear floor carpeting of the car.

Two days later, it was the morning of the big demonstration. Although the city's mayor had sworn that the city would provide no law enforcement support, almost two hundred riot-equipped police officers showed up around the park early that morning. They were aggressive inner city cops itching for a fight. An additional fifty U.S. Park Police from Washington and New York City had also been brought in. I was left with my partner, sitting in surveillance on the superintendent's house. We were disappointed that after the adrenaline rush of finding the possible bomber, we would miss out on all the action of the demonstration.

Everyone waited in nervous anticipation of what would happen. The permit was for ten o'clock that morning, and crowds of angry spectators began to fill the neighborhoods and streets surrounding the park. Ten o'clock came and went. By noon, it was looking like our demonstrators were not going to show. The crowds started to break up and move on, looking for some other entertainment.

It was later discovered by the FBI that the permit request had been a hoax. The individual who made the application had been kicked out of a Jewish defense group for being too radical. This whole scheme was intended to enflame the Jewish community into providing more emotional and financial support for Israel. It had worked, and the uproar of the media coverage echoed through the city for days.

As for the superintendent, he finally saw some value in having rangers trained and authorized to conduct law enforcement duties in his park. Furthermore, after this incident, he never again took issue with rangers wearing firearms. It is interesting how personal experience can shape a person's decision-making process.

Rangers and managers continued to wrangle over the wearing of firearms and other defensive equipment, such as handcuffs, batons, and such, for years. Superintendents have overall authority to interpret policy and guidelines for their individual park operations. They are much like the captain of a ship and do not often answer to higher authority. It was not until the 1990s when firm, written directives from the Washington agency headquarters prohibited deviation from policy, specifying that if law enforcement commissioned rangers were conducting law enforcement duties they would be armed, did this controversy find some rest. However, many managers did not embrace this strong language and were never able to adjust to this challenge to their omnipotent authority. This policy was then backed by further directives placing full responsibility for managing a safe and effective law enforcement program on superintendents within their parks. This meant that if anything went wrong, the accountability fell on their shoulders. At that point, superintendents began on the hard road to accepting this responsibility.

Today rangers receive the most intense and professional law enforcement training in the history of the agency. This includes eighteen weeks of training at the Federal Law Enforcement Training Center near Brunswick, Georgia, followed by a three-month field training program working with experienced and successful rangers in the parks. These highly trained professionals are then returned to their duty stations to start their career in upholding national park protection of visitors and resources for the enjoyment and education of future generations.

A course has also been developed for park superintendents at the Federal Law Enforcement Training Center, entitled "Law Enforcement for Managers." The course is only one-week long and is not required. Accountability is increasing, but changing almost one hundred years of organizational culture does not come easily.

Budgets

Working for the National Park Service is very similar to most federal, local, and state governments. Every service and the capacity to meet any legislated responsibility are dependent on money in the form of budgets. If there are insufficient funds to pay the bills or to hire personnel, the quality of the job accomplished diminishes. Then when times get flush, it becomes a challenge to use those suddenly available funds in an efficient and productive way. Managers are often forced to make decisions that seem odd or ineffective in order to save money and to stay within their budgets.

In 1979 I was working as a field ranger at Fredericksburg and Spotsylvania National Military Park. That year, budgets were cut in order to reduce the size of government expenditures, and fuel prices went up, with the price for a gallon of gas jumping from $2.00 to $3.29 per gallon (in 2009 dollars). This placed a burden on parks attempting to keep their vehicle fleets running. At Fredericksburg, determined to cut fuel consumption, the superintendent developed a plan to limit the gallons of fuel used in park ranger patrol vehicles. At the time, I was issued a Plymouth Gran Fury with a 440 Magnum four-barrel carburetor engine. The gas mileage was nothing to brag about, but that was common at that time. The plan called for me not to use more than thirty gallons of fuel per month. This allotment permitted me to cover the area I was responsible for, in the Fredericksburg Battlefield, two or three times per week. If there were any emergencies or call-outs at night, my gas budget would be shot for the month. One particular month, for the lack of fuel I went for two weeks without driving the car. I was not even able to drive from my residence to my office, which was five miles away. So I spent a lot of time sitting in my boss's office and conducting foot patrol at Chatham Manor, where my wife and I lived in the caretaker's cottage. One of the other rangers I worked with had to respond to several emergency calls, and he ran over his allotted fuel for the month. This was subtracted from his gas for the next month, leaving him with only twenty-five gallons that he could use.

The other part of this plan that was difficult to understand was that the law enforcement rangers were the only employees who had restrictions on their fuel consumption. The historians and maintenance divisions were still driving without concern for fuel. I remember on one of the days when I could get out in my government vehicle, the maintenance crew was putting in a sign along the road. There were three employees and three trucks, which they had driven for a total of forty miles round-trip, to do this simple job. Their lack of conservation was driving the rangers over the edge, and their morale was low. The perceived message was that the superintendent did not value the work done by his protection staff.

It did not take long for problems such as vandalism and damage to historic entrenchments to be identified by other employees. This result was blamed on the rangers, for not doing their jobs adequately to stop these illegal activities. No one put together that this increase in vandalism could be due to the lack of the presence of rangers enforcing regulations within the park. Costs for the repair of signs and for picking up litter were increasing, and we tried to explain that keeping the rangers parked without transportation hampered them from doing their jobs.

We continued under these conditions until the superintendent transferred to another park, and an acting replacement was sent from the Washington office. Our new acting superintendent was quick to find out about the fuel restrictions for the rangers and could not understand why other divisions within the park were not also conserving. He did some basic math and found that this false economy was costing the park money. A new plan was developed that restricted fuel use by the maintenance and interpretive divisions. They were required to plan out work ahead of time and to pool resources to limit the number vehicles used. The acting superintendent even gave up his government vehicle and used his personal car at his own expense. When examined at the end of the year, it was found that the park was saving more fuel with the new plan than when just the rangers were restricted. Vandalism also declined, which helped in preserving the park's irreplaceable resources.

In 1982 again the park service was faced with cuts in budgets and a government-wide push to conserve fuel. This started a program where only smaller--engine vehicles were available for agency use. On the Blue Ridge Parkway, the vehicle replacements that were delivered turned out to be Ford Fairmont sedans. Most had small four-cylinder engines that were extremely weak and inefficient in the mountainous terrain of the Southern Appalachians.

I was issued a robin's egg blue, four-cylinder Ford Fairmont. It had little or no acceleration or power. One of the first changes I had to make was to reduce the amount of equipment I carried in the car by at least half of what a park ranger normally carried. This made it more difficult to do the job when the tools needed were fifty miles away at the office. I vividly remember pulling into an overlook filled with more than fifty motorcycle gang members, who were drinking beer and throwing their cans over the side of the mountain. As I unfolded my six-foot, four-inch frame from the front seat of the tiny, blue Ford Fairmont, they broke into laughter, pointing at me. This destroyed any command presence I may have had to gain control of the situation. I ended up leaving for my own safety and had to call for assistance from the State Highway Patrol and the County Sheriff's Department.

I will never forget the day during hunting season when I

noted a pickup truck parked in a spot just off the parkway that was often used by illegal hunters. I drove my Fairmont down the steep access road and pulled in behind the pickup. Once I finished checking the situation out, finding that I had a hiker and not a hunter, I turned the car around and tried to pull up the hill, back onto the parkway. The engine roared, the transmission whined, and smoke started to pour out of the tailpipe, but the car could not make it back up the short hill to the main road. I tried backing up to get a running start twice, but I could only make it to twenty-five feet short of the stop sign at the parkway. I ended up driving almost thirty miles around on state roads to another access point to get back into the park.

Under the mountainous driving conditions that we subjected these cars to, the promised fuel economy was not there. The engines and transmissions had to work so hard to climb and descend mountain roads that the actual mileage was almost the same as the full-sized Ford and Chevy sedans we previously had.

Two years later, I was driving another Ford Fairmont when there was a report of a multiple-car accident at Mount Mitchell State Park near Asheville, North Carolina. Mount Mitchell is the highest peak east of the Mississippi, and it is a steep climb up the Blue Ridge Parkway to its entrance road. I had my Fairmont screaming, with my foot all the way to the floorboard, my emergency lights running, and siren blaring. As I went up the side of the mountain, visitors were passing me legally, as I was going five miles under the speed limit. After that, I told people that we had blue lights on the cars to keep people from running into our rear ends.

In addition to these inefficiencies, it soon became apparent that these vehicles were much more expensive to maintain. The cost saved in fuel, which was nowhere near what was projected, was greatly exceeded by the money spent to replace brakes, transmissions, and blown engines. By 1984, the National Park Service was able to go back to ordering more traditional law enforcement vehicles, including the full-sized Ford Crown Victoria and Chevy Caprice. Although the initial purchase cost increased, the overall operating cost and the length of service improved. The worst result of the false savings from this fuel conservation decision was the increased time it added to emergency responses and the lack of preparedness to handle incidents in remote areas due to lack of the emergency equipment, such as oxygen, firefighting gear, and tools, being immediately available. Efficiency and safety were sacrificed for budgetary concerns.

Another time, the budget was projected to contain large deficits, compared with the previous year. The decision was made not to hire temporary employees who normally started in April and early May until the middle of June. The small full-time staff ended up having to take care of the jobs normally covered by these employees. These included collecting fees in the campgrounds and manning information desks in visitor centers. The park's chief ranger told me that this was a good idea, and that it would prevent rangers from just riding up and down the road, burning gas. This changing of duties to save money was seen as a great success by the park superintendent. That summer, the number of visitors killed in the park tripled over the level of the past three years. Most of these deaths were the result of motor vehicle accidents. By September, the regional office in Atlanta wanted to know what was going on, and what was causing this increase in visitor fatalities. Suddenly, the park's management team was able to find funds enough to require that all law enforcement rangers work two hours overtime every day. Once the decision was made to get park rangers out into the park, there were no more fatalities in that visitor season.

Some years, it becomes difficult to impossible for parks to meet their payroll. Several times as a supervisor on the Blue Ridge Parkway I had to lay off seasonal employees for a month or more before the planned end of their work period because of lack of funding. This always occurred at the end of the season, during October, which is the most visited month of the year. The concern to meet payroll was such that I would not put myself in for overtime so that I would have funds available to pay my employees. I kept track in a calendar book of the hours I actually worked for three years. In one year, I worked almost 542 hours that I did not get paid for. That works out to be more than sixty-seven days of work that I "volunteered" to the National Park Service. I know there were others who worked even more free hours, due to their dedication to accomplish the mission of the National Park Service.

Games are played at higher political levels with budgets all the time. At one point, the Blue Ridge Parkway alone had sixty-plus permanent full-time positions vacant due to the lack of budgetary funds. When citizens asked their congressional representatives about the park's financial deficit, they were told that $3.2 million had been added to the park budget the year before. What they did not say was that this money was for the construction of a Western North Carolina Destination Center in Asheville, North Carolina. These funds could not be used for any other purpose and did not include the money to maintain and staff this new facility. The money budgeted did not include the funds for hooking up the new building to utilities. This had to be paid out of the park operating budget at a cost near $100,000. The utility bills and maintenance of the building in addition to staffing the information desk now have to be paid on a continuing basis out of the park budget. As a result, this new facility became more of a strain on the park's limited resources than any help, resulting in a cut in personnel and services in other areas of the park.

In 2008, the Blue Ridge Parkway received over a million dollars in what was called Centennial Funding. This program was designed to help the parks to get ready for the one-hundredth anniversary of the National Park Service. This funding was announced just prior to a presidential election, to show support for national parks. When the funding showed up at the Blue Ridge Parkway, it could only be used for hiring seasonal temporary employees; permanent salaries could not be paid, nor could the funding be used for supplies and equipment or for utility bills. This infusion of funding was only for that one year and could not be used to deal with any long-term or more serious problems facing the park. Then the assessments started roll in. These are charges taken from individual park budgets to pay for unfunded programs such as regional offices, IT systems, and emergencies. The final result was that the assessments exceeded the Centennial Funds. So the park ended up with less real dollars than the year before and a significant amount of funds that could only be used for hiring temporary employees. In the meantime, the politicians were able to run their election campaigns, showcasing all the money they had pumped into improving the National Park Service budget.

The bottom line of this story is that during my thirty-three years with the National Park Service, there was never enough money budgeted to properly manage and accomplish the job as expected by congress and the public. Individual, dedicated employees continue to fulfill their responsibilities but also continue to work in conditions hindered by lack of financial backing to provide staffing and safe, up-to-date equipment. As visitation, encroachments on park boundaries, and outside environmental changes affect our parks, minimal budgets often developed for political rather than realistic, mission-driven objectives contribute to the degradation and demise of our national parks.

The Traveling Ranger

Working for a federal agency such as the National Park Service, rangers often have to travel all over the country for special work details such as fighting fires, rendering aid in natural disasters, attending major special events in parks, preparing for presidential visits to parks, and for training. I will never forget a trip I made from Virginia to Arizona to attend a training course in the Grand Canyon.

I was working at the Fredericksburg and Spotsylvania National Military Park in 1979 when I received the opportunity to participate in what was known as ranger skills training. This was a six-week course that forms basic training for park rangers. During that time rangers are exposed to as many facets of national park operations as possible, including resource protection, communications, education, firefighting, safety, resource management, supervision, planning, public speaking, and presentations, just to name part of the curriculum. This was a difficult course to get into, since it was in such demand for new rangers, and I was honored to find out I was going.

What further added to the excitement was that the course was conducted at the Horace Albright Training Center located at the Grand Canyon. When I received my formal written notification, it was accompanied by a three-page questionnaire, which requested, "list three reasons you want to take this course, list three goals you hope to obtain from this course," and it went on from there. I decided that the best thing to do was be honest: My three goals were to see the Grand Canyon, hike in the Grand Canyon, and camp in the Grand Canyon. I thought no one could make me pay for being totally honest. However, I did not realize what I was getting into by attempting to get to the Grand Canyon. I believe my trip there paid me back for being so sarcastically honest.

It all started when my supervisor informed me that I had to fly to the Grand Canyon on a "super saver fare" or I could not go. The problem was that I only had two weeks before leaving, and all the direct route super saver seats were booked. I literally spent hours on the phone trying to make some type of arrangements. Finally I had an itinerary lined up where I would fly from Washington, D.C., to Cincinnati, Ohio, then to Salt Lake City to spend the night. The next day I would fly from Utah to San Francisco and then to Phoenix, Arizona, and spend the night flying to the Grand Canyon the next day, with this next day being one day after the course had started. But, they were all super saver tickets.

I then went to my supervisor and showed him the travel plan, and he exploded, "Do you know how much it is going to cost for motel rooms for those two nights?" I mentioned the fact that he had said I could only go to the training if I had super savers. His answer was, "That is not what I meant." The next thing I knew I was ordered to reserve regular commercial seating. My boss, the chief ranger, was still not very happy.

At least I was finally going to be on my way. My wife dropped me off at the airport, and my first stop was Chicago. There I transferred to a DC-10 Jumbo Jet. Not long before this, there had been a terrible crash of a DC-10 at the Chicago O'Hare Airport, and all DC-10s were to be grounded for an extended inspection period. When I boarded my connecting flight and reviewed the emergency escape route booklet from the seatback in front of me (after checking for the stomach distress bag), I was shocked to realize I was on board a DC-10. I flagged down the flight attendant as she floated by, and told her that I could have sworn these aircraft were grounded. She perkily informed me, "Oh, no, sir. We were just cleared to fly this morning. In fact, this will be the first DC-10 flight our airline has had since the grounding." Boy, did I feel confident. This flight was bound for Las Vegas, and I figured everybody on board but me must be a gambler anyway, and I was right.

As the plane began to fill up, I noticed a man working his way up the aisle. He was short and slender with a high hair line and what hair was left was a thinning salt and pepper color. As he got closer, I noticed he had a bright sparkle in his eyes and seemed to be bouncing on the balls of his feet, even as he was working his way through the shoulder-to shoulder-people and their luggage. What really struck me as he came closer was his outfit. He had numerous gold chains around his neck and a bright-colored nylon shirt with dice printed all over it, open to his navel. His pants were a dark-colored double knit, accented by white socks and black loafers. As he kept coming in my direction I found myself staring at what I supposed was my first real Las Vegas gambler. Suddenly I was shaken from my revelry by his high-pitched, cracked voice saying, "Hey bub, looks like we're seatmates."

The flight became at times an interesting rundown on all the casinos and gaming houses in Las Vegas. It seemed my new companion was a Chicago native who took a junket to Vegas three or four times a year. He was trying to come up with an angle to get his employers to move him there permanently. He was aghast to discover that I was on a plane bound for the gambling Mecca of the world with no intent to even step foot in a casino. "What the heck is there to do at the Grand Canyon? Stick with Vegas; it's a real happening place," he told me. I kindly listened to all his advice, which flowed constantly. He had a captive audience and knew it. The passenger on the other side of the man who became known to me as "The Gambler" had been smart enough to feign sleep from the moment the man had approached our aisle. I did get some respite when lunch was served. I recall The Gambler ate both his meal and that of our sleeping companion.

Finally, we arrived at the Las Vegas Airport. The Gambler

quickly grabbed his carry-on bag from under his seat and headed down the aisle. He had told me never to travel with more than a carry-on to Vegas, since "Luggage only slows you down." He was hitting the slot machines in the airport waiting area the last time I saw him. I was more than ready to start the next leg in my journey.

This was planned to be a flight on the famous Scenic Airlines to the Grand Canyon. Scenic Airlines runs small, twelve-passenger flights to smaller airports in the northern Arizona region. What distinguished their flights was that they were more of a "tour from the sky" than basic transportation. The stories of buzzing famous landmarks as if barnstorming with the Red Baron while making strafing runs were legendary. The number of passengers that got air sick was also legendary. I approached the check-in desk only to discover that the flights to the Grand Canyon had been canceled due to snow at higher elevations. I looked around me and found eleven other lost-looking souls. With a few quick questions, I found they were fellow students in the same ranger class, also trying to get to the Grand Canyon.

Now, we were not normal, stranded travelers. We were government employees on official travel status and tied down with all the restrictions and regulations that a major bureaucracy can produce. I went to find out about the possibility of renting a van, and some others called the training center for instructions. We were informed that we could not rent vehicles since our travel authorizations did not permit it, and since we were already traveling this could not be changed. After about an hour of additional calling back and forth it was decided that we would take a Greyhound bus leaving at midnight from downtown Las Vegas to Flagstaff, Arizona, where vans from the training center would meet us. Now we had to get twelve people, and all their luggage and camping gear for a six-week stay, to downtown Las Vegas.

Two group members were volunteered as negotiators and sent out in search of an airport limo service van to take us to the bus station. They returned and said we would be picked up in about fifteen minutes, and then they quickly disappeared on personal errands. We gathered our luggage into a small mountain just outside the door and waited for a van to show up. A few minutes later two long, black stretch limos pulled up, and the uniformed drivers exited and began to talk amongst themselves. I was still guarding our gear and waiting for the van while everyone else hid in the air-conditioned terminal. Finally, one of the drivers approached me and asked, "Are you with the park rangers trying to get to the Grand Canyon?"

"Yeah."

He got a big smile on his face, showing a whole mouth of perfect teeth, and said, "We're the limos to take you to the bus station." I stood there, dumbfounded.

As it turned out, our negotiators had no idea of what an airport limo service was and instead rented two limousines to take us to the bus station. The drivers told us that they normally drive around people such as Frank Sinatra, Cher, and other celebrities, but they thought it was pretty funny when these two guys wanted to rent a limo to go to the bus station. After quite a bit of effort of tying stretched bungee cords and string, we got our entire luggage mountain into the two limos and took off. We got a first-class tour of downtown Las Vegas and finally ended up at the bus station at the end of the famous Vegas Strip. The two drivers thought the whole situation was so ridiculous that they did not even charge us for the ride.

Once we had our bus tickets purchased and our luggage stored in lockers, we hit the streets of Vegas. None of our group had been there before, so this was a new experience for everyone. We had about twelve hours until the bus left. I had already been traveling for fourteen hours, as had several other members of the group. Nobody had much money, so we decided that we would rent a motel room that we all could share, taking naps in shifts. We did not believe that any motel desk clerk in their right mind would rent a room to a group of twelve people, even in Las Vegas, so a male and female member of the group were selected to go and rent the room. They entered the lobby and stepped up to the desk while four of us (the first shift) stood outside watching through the window. The "couple" turned and entered the elevator and we waited about ten minutes before approaching the desk. It did not take long for our plans to fall apart. I asked the lady behind the desk for the room number of the couple that had just checked in, since we were friends of theirs. She looked at me suspiciously and asked, "And what were their names?"

I froze. We had only met an hour or so before and their names were lost somewhere between my brain and tongue. Luckily another group member behind me chimed in with "Doug Cookson." The desk clerk looked at us suspiciously over her reading glasses as if she was trying to decide if we were here to make a "hit" or a drug buy. She picked up the desk phone and dialed a number. I was ready to bolt for the door if the number she dialed was 911. "Hello, Mrs. Cookson?"

There was a great, silent pause and I could hear the sound of wheels turning on the other end of the phone. The female member of our group upstairs had also forgotten the name of the person she was with. Finally, she responded, "Oh, yeah!" And I got another look from the clerk.

"There are some friends of yours here at the desk. Should I send them up to your room?" There was some indiscernible answer, and she hung up the phone. "They are in room 408. You can use the elevator over there." With quick thanks, we were on our way. After this experience, I knew I did not have the nerves to be a criminal.

We finally got to our room, which was about the size of a walk-in closet. "Mr. and Mrs. Cookson" left for the casinos, and the first shift prepared to sleep for three hours. I ended up on the floor between the bed and window in a space about one and a half feet wide. We had turned out the lights and closed the blinds when we learned that the side of the motel where our room was located was directly across the street from the Las Vegas Hospital's emergency room. Sirens were heard in intervals of five to eight minutes. I know this because I laid there on the hard floor timing them for three hours.

Mercifully, my shift in the room ended and our group hit

the streets. We had about eight hours until the bus was scheduled to leave. We spent this time visiting casinos on the strip,
where we played slot machines and black jack. We did discover
one benefit of gambling. In the casinos, they have lovely young
ladies that walk around with trays of mixed drinks. They were
giving drinks out for free to gamblers. I soon learned that by
positioning myself on a proper slot machine and putting in a
quarter as the waitress turned the corner, I could get all the free
drinks I wanted. This was entertaining for about an hour.

By eleven-thirty I was starting to wear down, so I headed
for the bus station. To my surprise the station which had been
empty earlier when we bought our tickets was now full, stand-
ing-room only. As I looked around the lobby I saw several members of our group mixed in with a real assortment of characters.
Some looked like they had probably flown into town first class
but due to the outcome of their fortunes were taking the Greyhound bus home. In one corner was a crowd of Native Americans passing around bottles in bags. Every once in a while one
would jump up and yell something at one of the others. This
person would jump up and scream something back, and the
clerk from behind the desk would lean out and shout for both
of them to shut up and sit down. I felt as if I were watching a
scene from a 1950s B movie, except this one was in color.

A call was made for a bus leaving for Los Angeles, and quite
a few people got up and moved in line toward the rear door. I
was able to find a seat as more people poured in from the front
entrance of the station. As I tried to make myself comfortable in
a round, hard, plastic seat, I looked across the aisle at a member
of my ranger class named Mike and a woman who was taking
a seat next to him. The woman appeared to be anywhere from
fifty to eighty-five years old. She was dressed in a faded and
worn flower-print dress with knee-high support hose rolled
down around her ankles. A knit cap was on her head that looked
like its main job was to keep her hair from falling off. She was
carrying a large shopping bag that was bulging full, and she sat
down with a great sigh as if she were exhausted from trying to
sleep next to a hospital emergency room.

Mike kept giving her sidewise glances as it appeared that she was mumbling to herself as she rocked back and forth in her seat. She finally turned and looked right into Mike's eyes, poked him in the ribs, and said clear as day, "Hey. It takes two to tango. You know what I mean." And she poked him again. With a look of shock on his face, Mike got up in search of another place to sit.

Within thirty seconds another man took the seat next to the woman, and the same scene was played out again with the man getting up and moving away. Finally, one of the Native Americans who had been arguing and making noise came over and sat in the seat to get away from his friends. Again the woman started with the rocking and mumbling and leaned over and poked him in the ribs and said, "Hey. It takes two to tango. You know what I mean?"

The man just looked back at her and said, "Yeah, I know what you mean, lady." The woman just went back to her mumbling and rocking. I was sitting there thinking that these two must be from the same reservation when the loudspeaker announced, "Bus twenty-nine to Flagstaff and Albuquerque loading at gate 2," which was odd, since there seemed to be only one gate. As people responded to this call I, noticed that the group of Native Americans got up and the "Tango Dancer" also moved toward the gate. The driver stood by the door of the bus and took tickets as passengers passed. When he got to the person in front of me he said, "Sorry, we're all filled up. You'll have to wait for the next bus tomorrow." There were five of us still not on the bus, and I was mad. The driver finally went on the bus to count seats and came back down to inform us that he found five extra seats. I am still not sure where they came from.

I entered the bus in the dark and noted that the Native Americans were all in the back with their bottles still being passed around and singing what sounded like "A Hundred Bottles of Beer on the Wall" in Navajo. The bag lady "Tango Dancer" was sitting in the front seat to the right of the bus driver. I finally found an aisle seat about four rows back and collapsed.

The bus started to move, and as we entered the relaxing

darkness of the desert, the bus quieted, and I started to doze off. The next thing I knew I was shocked awake when all the lights along the luggage racks inside the bus came on and the driver announced over the public address system, "We are now approaching Hoover Dam, and I thought you all might want to see it." It was a spectacular sight to see Hoover Dam in all its floodlighted glory at one o'clock in the morning through heavy eyelids. Finally, the lights went out, and I started to nod off again.

I opened my eyes some undetermined time later and looked out through the front windshield of the bus. We were now at higher elevation, and snow was everywhere. I could not see how the driver could make out where he was going when the snow was so thick. I could not see the lanes of the interstate highway ahead of us. But as they say with Greyhound, "leave the driving to us," and I closed my eyes.

The next thing I knew I was awakened by the sound of air brakes. I looked out and the snow was gone. We were surrounded by desert and there was not a building or light to be seen anywhere. The bus slowed and came to a stop. With a rush of air, the doors opened. The Tango Dancer got up from her seat, grabbed her bag, and without a sound exited down the steps and off the bus. The doors immediately closed, and the last thing I saw was this old lady with her shopping bag, standing there all alone in the middle of the desert. The only thing I could figure was that this was as far as she could afford a ticket. I was starting to think that the true destination of this bus was The Twilight Zone.

Again I tried to get some sleep, only to awaken with the bus once again flying through the snow. As I looked through the windshield, I could not see the roadway in front of us and was wondering how the driver was navigating. Up ahead I could see some type of blinking light. As we got closer, I could tell it was an amber light that we were hurdling toward, and as we got even closer, I could make out that the blinking light was on a giant snow blower clearing the interstate. No sooner had I realized what we were approaching then we were passing it, as if it were standing still. After this experience I had an even harder time trying to sleep, but I started to drift, exhaustion taking its toll.

Once more I was startled awake by the sound of air brakes. The snow was gone again, and I noted that I was still alive. We approached an exit ramp and slowed for an approach. It was still pitch dark, and we came off the ramp into what looked like a deserted ghost town of dark and rundown buildings. The driver spent ten minutes maneuvering the bus around the narrow, dirt-packed streets until he came to a stop in front of a small house; he then opened the bus doors and jumped out. I leaned across my seat companion, who had not awakened since we left Las Vegas, and peered out the bus's side window. There the driver stood, in the front lawn of the house, relieving himself. He finished his duty, jumped back on the bus, and we headed back to the interstate. I figured that he did not want to take a chance on awakening the Native Americans in the back by getting to the rest room, or maybe the house belonged to a person he really did not care for.

As dawn finally approach on the horizon, the driver announced, "We will be stopping shortly in Kingman. Those of you going to Flagstaff will have to change busses at that point." Finally, I was going to get off this bus from hell and see some civilization. We found a one-room bus station, with four plastic seats and two vending machines. There was no time to find any other source of food. We all headed to the rest room. There, we found a man with a weathered and wrinkled southwestern face, slowly rubbing on the sinks with a rag. He was wearing what must have been a twenty-gallon hat, a silk, western-style multicolored shirt with fringe, polyester western-style pants, lizard skin boots, and, what really got my attention, a round ornate belt buckle the size of a large serving platter. He never looked up, but just kept rubbing that sink. Fifteen minutes later, I went back to the rest room one last time before the bus left, and he was still standing there, rubbing that same sink. I had to ask the clerk behind the desk who this guy was in the bathroom. He told me, "Oh, he's our janitor. The bus line pays him by the hour." I have always wondered how long it took him to finish that sink.

The bus ride from Kingman to Flagstaff was pretty uneventful. This bus was much less crowded and more comfortable. Besides, it was daylight, and things seemed much more real. We finally pulled into Flagstaff around ten o'clock in the morning, where two vans from the Training Center awaited us. The van drivers were all in a tizzy, since our bus was late, and we had to get to the center as soon as possible because classes were to have started that morning. They were not even going to let us stop for some breakfast until we threatened a mutiny.

When we finally arrived at the Albright Training Center, we were met on the sidewalk by a staff member who quickly herded us into the lobby. There we were issued room keys, told to place our luggage in the assigned rooms, and then report immediately to the classroom. I exclaimed in exhausted exasperation, "You have got to be kidding."

"No. We are already starting late and are going to have to go until ten o'clock tonight to make up for lost time."

That is what we did, and it was probably the first time that they had twelve people sleep through that much class time.

Lives

People's lives are an important part of being a park ranger. Rangers touch lives in so many ways, varying from the small school-age child, whose first experience of their cultural or natural heritage is through a program or walk given by a ranger, to the person whose life is saved from hanging by a thin thread of rope off a cliff. Without really paying attention as park rangers, we often never realize how these lives also touch us.

It was one hot, summer day on the Blue Ridge Parkway, and as was my habit, I stopped by a local country store that was just outside the park for a drink and some conversation. It always amazed me how much information you could pick up by spending a little time listening to the locals in these traditional gathering places. You could learn about how the weather was affecting farmers' crops, the current cattle prices, who was going to be the next president, and down to who was doing what to who and maybe who was doing what in the park. Several times I had people follow me out to my car to give me some juicy inside information on illegal activities.

On this particular hot, summer afternoon things were pretty quiet at the store. Only two or three local old-timers in their dust-covered bib overalls were sitting inside the door, trying to top each other with what latest gossip they knew. I went to the cooler in the back and lingered at the open door, lapping in the luxury of its refrigerated air, shopping for just what drink I wanted that day, when a small boy and his dad came in. The father looked hot and harried, like he had was slowly approaching the end of a hard day of parenting. The boy was full of energy and saying hello to everyone.

Near the cool, back of the store was a barrel of apples, which caught the boy's eye, and he zeroed in on it immediately. He ran over and picked up a choice selection and held it up admiringly to his dad and asked if he could have it. The father looked back over his shoulder to the other men and looked down at his son and softly whispered, "Son, you know we don't have no money." The boy dejectedly put the apple back in the barrel and wandered away to look at the candy display.

I was still standing with my head in the cooler, making my final selection, when I had overheard this quick exchange. I picked up my drink, which was the same one that I always got at that store, and went to the counter. The father was with the other locals, making his information exchange, which must have been the reason for the trip to the store. I put my drink on the counter, and when the owner asked, "Will there be anything else?," I replied in a conspiratorial whisper, "Yeah, I'll pay for an apple for that boy."

The owner nodded his head in approval, and I paid my bill. I was out front just getting ready to get into my car when I heard the screen door on the store slam. I turned around, and there was the boy running toward me with one of the biggest smiles and one of the biggest apples I had ever seen. He just ran up to me and said, "Thank you, ranger, for the apple." I just said, "You're welcome," as I got in my car and went back to work.

My wife taught school in the local town, and a month and a half later when she returned to work she had a boy she had never seen before in her class come up to her. The boy stood with his back straight and his chest pumped out and told her how her husband the park ranger had bought him an apple at the store one day. She came home that night and asked me about it, and I told her the story.

You know, that was more than twenty-five years ago, and I can still see that boy's smile. I think I always will.

That is just an example of the positive experiences and impacts that can be had during a career as a park ranger. But, unfortunately, there are also many horrendous experiences and scenes that you are exposed to that stick with you through the rest of your life. These instances of dealing with real-world life and death were not what I considered when I became a national park ranger in 1975. Little did I know that I would have to repeatedly respond to human fatalities, murders, and scenes of child abuse and notify family members of the death of their loved ones.

My first such family notification was probably my most difficult. It was in 1979, while working at the Fredericksburg and Spotsylvania National Military Park in Virginia. A group of students from Spotsylvania High School decided to play hooky one day, and in the course of their celebrating they got ahold of some beer and got drunk. They were riding around in an old pickup truck that belonged to one of the boys. At one point while in the Spotsylvania battlefield, they decided to let a fifteen-year-old girl, who had also been drinking, try driving the truck. It was a manual transmission, and she was having trouble shifting gears. The sixteen-year-old boy who owned the truck was riding in the truck's bed and leaned over the driver's side window to help direct the girl's driving. At that inopportune point she drove the truck off the left-hand side of the road, into a forested road shoulder. The boy struck his head against a tree, crushing his right side and killing him instantly. The kids scrambled around, hiding all the beer cans, and had some friends in another car take the girl driver home.

The duty fell to me as the investigating ranger to contact the family and inform them of the death of their son. I had received little or no training in such matters, and my supervisor declined to accompany me in this task. The county sheriff knew the family and agreed to lead me to their home. When I arrived, the door was answered by the boy's father. I thought the best approach with such horrible news was to be direct. I simply told him that there had been an accident, and we had some bad news. He stood there staring at me with a fearful look on his face and asked me if his son was hurt. With a quivering voice I was able to get out, "No, I am afraid he has been killed." I thought the man would collapse as the wind leaked out of him. He pulled himself back up and asked me to break the news to his wife since he could not. He took me to a backroom on the first floor, where a woman who had obviously been very ill for a long time was propped up in a bed. We were told later that she was dying of cancer and had only been given a few months to live. I again delivered my tragic news. I thought my knees were going to give out, having to tell this dying woman that her teenage son preceded her in death. She immediately fell apart and started screaming and thrashing, pulling the IV tubes from her arm.

About that time, several other friends and neighbors arrived, after seeing our patrol cars outside and fearing the worst. We all sat together with the devastated parents and cried. They wanted to know all the details of what had happened, but I could not tell them much since the students involved had not been very forthright in giving any information.

When I had arrived at the gruesome crash scene, no one claimed to know who was driving the truck. It was not until days later that guilt finally got to one of the other girls, and she told me who the driver had been. Eventually the girl that was driving was charged with manslaughter in juvenile court but was never convicted. Years later, there were several civil cases that resulted in large amounts of money moving between insurance companies, but very little went to the family devastated by this loss.

Although I could never know the grief and pain of this loss for this family, this incident had significant impact on me. For years I would have dreams where I would see that mother sitting in that bed, and I would have to tell her again about her son. Unfortunately, this was not the only time I had to be the bearer of tragic news. Each time I became involved in such notifications, I thought back to that first experience.

In 1998, while working on the Blue Ridge Parkway, we received a report of a car fire at mile post 5. No law enforcement rangers were in the area, so two interpretive seasonal park rangers from the Humpback Rocks Visitor Center responded in their personal cars. When they arrived, they were shocked to find not only a burning car, but a burning body behind the steering wheel. When I arrived, everyone on scene seemed to be in shock and unable to move. The car was still in flames, and the odor of burning flesh was overpowering. The fire departments finally arrived and were able to put out the flames.

At this point I had been involved in hundreds of motor vehicle crashes and had never seen a car burn like this one. Once the vehicle had cooled off we found two exploded gas cans in the trunk. The medical examiner's office also found traces of accelerants on the victim's clothes, burned into what remained of the skin.

One of the license plates was still intact, and a computer check gave us a name and address in Charlottesville, Virginia. We went to the residence to talk to the family, even though we were not positive who was in the car. No one seemed to be at home. A neighbor came over to see what was going on. We were told that no one from the family was at home. The wife and daughter were with the high school band on a trip in Florida. The son was on a Cub Scout trip to the Blue Ridge Parkway and was to spend the next two nights there. The father was not on the trip and was supposed to be at work. The neighbor described the husband's vehicle, and it sounded like he could be our victim. We also learned that the husband worked at the University of Virginia's bookstore in Charlottesville. We then went to the University of Virginia Police Department and found that the man we were looking for was going to be fired from his job with the university and prosecuted for embezzlement of funds.

We were a bit stuck in that the body was burned beyond anyone being able to identify it. The body had burned so intensely that during the initial examination the medical examiner was unable to positively ascertain if it was male or female.

We did not want to tell a wife who was away on a trip with her daughter that her husband might be dead. We met with other family members, and they decided to wait until the wife arrived home to notify her. The other problem we had was trying to get a positive identification on our victim. We got the names of several dentists from other family members, but none had the husband as a patient, so we had no access to dental records for identification purposes.

Three days later, we met the high school band's bus in a local shopping center parking lot. With me were several family members, their church minister, and another ranger there for my moral support. In this case we stood in the background while the minister took the mother and her daughter aside and broke the bad news to them. She immediately fell to her knees and had to be caught and supported by three people. They eventually got her to a bench, and her sister informed me that she wanted to talk with me. I tried to explain as best I could (but leaving out the part about the fire) what we knew about what had happened to who we believed was her husband. She seemed assured that it was indeed her husband who had been in the car. Once she was able to collect herself, she was able to give us the name of her husband's dentist. It was this information that finally led us to make a positive identification of the body. It was indeed her husband.

As far as we could piece the circumstances together, the victim was despondent about being caught stealing at work. No one in his family was aware of this. He was fired and told that he would be charged after his wife left for the trip to Florida with their daughter. I believe that he came to the Blue Ridge Parkway, where his young son was on a Cub Scout hike, attempting to see his son one last time. We will never know if he did perhaps see the boy from a distance. Perhaps whatever happened in the park cemented his final decision to drive his car off the road headlong into a large tree. The vehicle fire was the result of the gasoline in the car's trunk. I remembered that the medical examiner had found fuel on the remains of his clothes. This led me to believe that the man had poured gasoline on himself and the interior of the car. That is what resulted in the extremely charred condition of his body.

In another instance, a young man committed suicide by driving his new car, with less than 1,000 miles on it, off the side of the mountain on the Blue Ridge Parkway. He was not discovered until early the next morning. Apparently his girl friend had broken up with him the day before, and he could not face it. Upon investigation, we found that the man was a recent graduate of the University of Virginia (less than an hour's drive away) and was working as a teacher at a local private school. He was originally from Jackson, Mississippi. We called the Jackson police department to see if they could assist us in contacting a family member.

Once I spoke to a dispatcher and gave him the name, he became suddenly quiet and told me to hold on. About five minutes later an agitated voice came on the line, identifying himself as the chief of police. He told me that he knew the family personally and would make the contact for us. I gave him a basic outline of what we knew, and then he switched me over to one of his detectives to get more details. The detective then began to grill me and question our investigation and wanted to know who I was and what experience I had in such matters. I had finally had enough and said, "Wow, wait a minute. What is going on here? I have never seen a reaction like this to a request for family notification."

The detective then explained to me that the victim was the only son of one of the oldest, wealthiest, and politically connected families in Mississippi. We were finally winding down when I was put on hold again. When the detective picked back up again, he told me that the chief was with the family at their home, so notification had been made. I gave him my contact numbers and was finally permitted to get on with my work.

The next morning I arrived in my office to five messages from the same detective. When I called him back he informed me that the family's pilot would be coming in to the closest airport and would meet with me for a briefing and to attend the autopsy with me in Richmond. I met the private jet at the

Weyers Cave airport that afternoon and was presented with a very official looking legal document authorizing the pilot to represent the family in all aspects related to their son's death. There was also a request signed by the Jackson chief of police, requesting the courtesy of allowing the pilot to attend the autopsy. A quick telephone check with the U.S. attorney's office gave permission for the pilot to accompany me. I was grilled by the pilot all the way to Richmond. He was not very forthcoming in providing any information back, so I finally started running out of answers. After some silence broken only by the sound of the road, he told me that he was a retired federal agent and had worked a lot of investigations before. When I asked him what agency he worked for, he was very elusive and indirect. I had learned enough over the years to know that this usually meant the CIA or some other security agency. I started to wonder what else this guy did for the family.

The circumstances of this death were confirmed by the medical examiner. The young man had died as the result of loss of blood directly caused by his injuries. He had left a suicide note in the car and in his apartment at the school where he taught.

I drove the pilot back to his plane. The only comment he made on the hour and a half drive back was, "He had never had to deal with disappoint in his life." Being dumped by his girl friend was probably more than this young man could handle.

Unfortunately, suicides happen quite frequently in national parks and specifically on the Blue Ridge Parkway. I had a counselor tell me one time that when people reach the decision to end their lives, they often go to a place where they have fond memories, where it is peaceful, and where they know they will be found. This could easily explain the number of such incidents on the parkway.

I was in the office at James River on the Blue Ridge Parkway one day, when the administrative assistant asked me to take a telephone call that had just come in. "This lady sounds a bit strange and maybe you should talk to her."

I picked up the phone, identified myself, and asked what I could do to help. The woman at the other end of the line then asked, "How often do your rangers patrol the overlooks on the parkway?"

I was puzzled as to the reason for the question. Was this someone contemplating a crime? Perhaps it was someone from the media wanting to publish a story that would make us susceptible to criminal activity. Or more likely this was someone wanting information to back up some complaint. I decided to be direct and asked why she wanted to know.

The woman decided that I did not know who she was, so she poured her heart out to me. She was fighting depression and despair in her life and had decided to end it all by committing suicide in an overlook on the Blue Ridge Parkway. She was just concerned about how long her body would lay there before a park ranger would find her.

I knew that I would be unable to help this woman with her problems, and it was obvious that she had been thinking this through for some time, so I attempted another track and explained to her that we were very short-handed, which was true, and that it could be days before a ranger checked a specific overlook. I further explained that others had committed suicide in the park but normally it was not a ranger that found them. Typically, suicides were found by families that just happened to stop to enjoy the view and ended up finding a dead body there.

I could tell that this upset her plans, and she told me she would not want that to happen. I tried to get more information from her, and she eventually said she was sorry and hung up on me.

I immediately punched the buttons on the phone so it would record the telephone number that had last called in. It revealed a residential telephone number in the nearby city of Lynchburg, Virginia. I then called the Lynchburg Police Department and through their records got the woman's name and address. After I spoke to a detective, the police department sent an officer and a crisis counselor to the house. The detective called me the next day and informed me that they were able to make a positive intervention with the woman who had called me and that she was entered into a treatment program. I never heard any more about this woman, but I certainly hope that the intervention aided her in dealing with her problems.

One of the important lessons about life that I learned from these experiences and many others is that we never know what each day holds for us or for others. It can all end in the flash of a second. We need to keep this in mind and realize the effect we have on others. We can be a positive influence and help others in the minutest actions of our day. One minute of kindness or listening can change a person's life forever.

The Interstate Fugitive and The Hound Dog Rangers

Working in national parks, you never quite know what to expect. Because a park ranger is responsible for so many different functions, a situation can change dramatically at a moment's notice. Rangers are often alone or perhaps with one partner and are long distances from any assistance. It is not unusual to sit and wait for hours for any type of help to arrive when a situation has gone bad. As a result, you really have to depend on the people you work with and on other agencies for assistance. Things do not always work out as we might hope.

In 1982, I was working in a district of the Blue Ridge Parkway in North Carolina. There I worked closely with Harold Wood, one of the best field rangers I have ever been teamed up with. Harold had grown up in the shadow of the Great Smokey Mountains and spent most of his youth scaling steep, rocky slopes. As a result, it was a real challenge to keep up with him in the woods. I always felt like a racehorse on his last legs after a day in the woods with Harold. He would just take off up a slope that you would swear was as steep as the Empire State Building, and he'd keep going until he noticed you were not behind him. When you finally caught up to him leaning against a tree, not even breaking a sweat, Harold would take off on you again. It was a lot like trying to catch a jackrabbit with your legs tied together.

On this particular day we had worked an entire shift attempting to re-mark the park boundary in an area called Cumberland Knob. The slopes and rocks contained some of the most rugged terrain in the district. Harold and I mutually agreed that the next time this boundary would be posted was when a new team of rangers transferred in.

We were driving back toward the district office and approached an area called Mahogany Rock. At one time this had been a small subdivision located at the top of the mountain. There had been a cable car which ran from a large gravel parking lot to the next mountain, where a small restaurant had served hotdogs and sandwiches on a patio, which offered a fantastic view in all directions. The park service had bought this property with the intent of preserving the surrounding area from further development. All the buildings and the cable car system had been removed, leaving the park with the main road, the driveways, and a parking lot. Since the access road leading from the Blue Ridge Parkway was still listed as a state highway, we could not close the area off to vehicles. As a result, we had a ready-made parking spot in a somewhat remote area and experienced problems there with underage drinking, vandalism, fires, and littering. Mahogany Rock was well known throughout the area as a hang out and a meeting place for illicit activities.

As we approached the turn-off for Mahogany Rock, Harold suggested that we check it out. I was tired from chasing Harold all day up slopes that even a goat would have trouble with, and as usual at this time of day I was more concerned with what was for supper. Harold could be quite persuasive and gave me one of his looks that filled one with guilt about doing the right thing. Besides, there were about five more minutes until quitting time, anyway. With that, it was decided that I had better go along with Harold's instinct, and I pulled onto the access road.

When we arrived at what had been the parking lot for the cable car operation, we found an older model red van and a motor home parked across from us, with a group of people looking like they were going to set up camp for the night. Camping in this area was prohibited, so Harold walked over to the folks to inform them, in that ever diplomatic ranger style, that they had to pack up and leave the area. As I viewed the scene before me, a lightbulb started to flicker in my brain that there was something familiar about this group of people and their vehicles. As Harold spoke to a man and two women, a Siberian husky puppy ran around from behind the motor home. All of a sudden the signal light in my head started getting brighter, and I slipped back into my patrol car and started flipping through my notebook. Before long, there it was, from about three weeks before, a complete description of the happy campers before me, right down to the dog and the license plate on the van.

We had received a somewhat random call at our office from a dispatcher at an adjoining county sheriff's department. He informed us of a man who had escaped from their jail the previous day and who was traveling in a motor home or red van with two women and two young boys. There were outstanding arrest warrants on the man, identified as Johnny Orville Cole, in about six states for bad checks, larcenies, escaping from jail, and various other crimes. Cole was reported to be heavily armed, prone to violence, and he had sworn he would kill before he went back to prison. The point that stood out in the description was that one of the items this group had bought with a bad check was a Siberian husky puppy from a pet store in a shopping mall.

I felt my adrenalin start to pump, and Harold was still about fifty feet away from my car, chit-chatting with this desperado and his gang. I did not want to do anything to alarm the suspects with Harold right in the midst of them, so I waited as coolly as possible until Harold finished and walked back to our car. After he got in, I handed him my notes and pulled out of the parking lot. As Harold was reading, I contacted the park's dispatcher with the van and motor home's license plate numbers to run a computer check to ensure we were correct in identifying this crew. Suddenly Harold let out a loud, "Damn, and you let me stand right there with them?" I tried to assure Harold that, with my eagle eye expertise with a handgun, I could have gotten three rounds into Cole before he moved. This did not seem to reassure Harold.

About that time the dispatcher came back over the air to confirm that the license plate had come back as a hit, meaning it was wanted. The information he gave me was basically what I had gotten three weeks before. I then informed the dispatcher that we had the subjects under surveillance and to send us some backup and assistance from the state highway patrol or sheriff's department. Harold quickly got out of the car and grabbed the shotgun from the car's trunk, where we were required to carry it.

Suddenly the motor home and van came out of the parking lot and headed back down the access road toward the parkway. We did not feel safe stopping the vehicles by ourselves, so we decided to follow and keep them under observation until some backup arrived to assist. I called the dispatcher and informed him of this latest development and to check on when our assistance would arrive. He informed me that he had the Virginia State Police (we were in North Carolina) on the phone getting more information on the suspect. I quickly informed him that I did not need any more information but needed backup as soon as possible.

Cole was driving the motor home with one of the women following in the van. They got onto the parkway heading north. We fell in behind them and were all heading toward the Virginia state line, which was about fifteen miles away. We noticed that the van kept dropping back, leaving a large space between the motor home and itself. I felt that the van wanted us to pass it, but I did not feel safe getting sandwiched between the two of them, so we continued to follow them at a discreet distance.

I called the dispatcher back a third time to find out how close our assistance was. I was informed that an investigator from the Virginia State Police was on the phone and the dispatcher was attempting to arrange for someone to come down and identify Cole. At this point I became a bit upset and in a more direct manner said, "I don't need any more damn information, and we do not have this guy in custody for anyone to identify. What I need is some help down here."

To my relief a district ranger from another area was monitoring our conversation and called over the radio, telling me that he had the local sheriff's department on the phone and wanting to know where we needed them. A sense of reprieve came over me in that, finally, we might get some help. As this slight feeling of euphoria was settling in, both the motor home and van pulled off the parkway westbound on U.S. Route 21. Luckily, I thought, they were heading straight toward our backup that was supposed to be on the way to help get the vehicles stopped. As we followed them down the state road, both vehicles pulled into a small mom-and-pop style restaurant parking lot. We noticed that there were a number of people in the area returning to their cars after a meal. I did not feel safe pulling into the parking lot with all those people around for fear of provoking a confrontation with a reportedly heavily armed suspect (I have to admit that this aspect of the description we had was foremost in my mind). We drove slowly passed the van and motor home and went another quarter mile or less to the next intersection and turned around. As we approached the restaurant at a slow speed from the opposite direction, we found to our dismay that the two vehicles we had been following were now gone.

They could only have headed back toward the parkway, so I took off in that direction as fast as my vehicle could go. We had not gone far when a county sheriff's department deputy came up behind us with his lights and siren on. At that time we were unable to talk to any other agencies with our radios, so I had to pull over and explain as fast as I could the situation to the deputy. His reaction was in the frame of, "Why are you bothering me with this?" but I finally persuaded him to assist us in relocating these vehicles and their occupants. The direction they had apparently gone in would either take them back on the parkway or to another intersecting state road that paralleled the parkway going north toward Virginia. For some reason my gut feeling was that north and out of the state was where they were heading. The deputy reluctantly agreed to search the state road, and Harold and I took off for the parkway.

Although we did not have two-way radio communications with the sheriff's department, I did have a scanner in my car that enabled us to listen to their radio traffic. We had only gone a short distance north when we monitored that the deputy and a police officer from a nearby town had the van and motor home stopped at another small restaurant and country store on the state road. Both Harold and I were surprised to hear that the suspects had been found, and we left the park and flew to this location to now serve as backup for the county.

When we arrived, the red van was stopped at the entrance to a small country store. A woman and one of the children were outside the van. The motor home was stopped in the parking lot of a restaurant about fifty yards from the van. The deputy was sitting in his car with the door open and his left leg hanging out. Johnny Cole was standing in front of the deputy's open door with his hands on the window frame as we pulled up. Cole immediately took his hands off the door, and Harold jumped out with the shotgun. I ordered Cole to step back from the vehicle, and he started to protest, wanting to know what was going on. At that point the deputy slowly lumbered out of his car with a red face and started to lay into us for making such a big deal about nothing. He had run a computer check on the Michigan driver's license Cole had given him and the tag on the motor home, and everything was in order. The deputy was planning on releasing Cole when we pulled up. I tried to explain to the deputy that this person was indeed Johnny Orville Cole, and that he should not be released due to all the serious warrants out on him. I was really taking a long jump at this point due to our being out of our jurisdiction, but I knew beyond a doubt that this person was wanted and dangerous, and I was not going to let him just leave.

Cole then stated that he had additional identification in the motor home, and the deputy told him to go and get it. Harold instantly stepped between Cole and the motor home and told him, "No way am I going to let you into that vehicle." We then again tried to persuade the deputy to hold them until a Virginia State Police investigator arrived to ID him. The deputy became even more agitated and red-faced that we were stepping on his toes in handling this situation.

About this time the county sheriff himself arrived at the scene and stopped at the van. I told Harold to keep an eye on Cole, and I went to talk with the sheriff, whom I was sure would understand the situation. After listening to the now scarlet-faced deputy and me, the sheriff decided that he did not have anything to hold these people for, and since they had not committed a crime in his county, he felt they should be released. As the sheriff reached this conclusion I asked if anyone had obtained the identification of the woman driving the van or had looked through the vehicle. Everyone just looked at the ground, and I asked the woman for her driver's license, which appeared valid. Looking back toward the motor home I noted that the second woman had decided to come out and was now standing by Cole. On a whim, I used my portable radio and asked Harold to check the other woman's identity. She gave him her driver's license, which appeared to be in order. When we compared information it turned out that the two drivers' licenses from separate states were for the same name, date of birth, and social security number but had each respective woman's photo. In other words, both women claimed to be the same person. Even the sheriff had to admit that this seemed a bit odd. He then asked the woman for permission to look through the van. She said, "Sure, go ahead."

The sheriff took a quick look through the van and said that he did not find anything unusual other than quite a bit of electronics equipment and boxes in the back. I asked if it was alright if I looked through the vehicle, and the woman again gave verbal permission. I quickly found a loaded .357 magnum pistol, which had been hidden under the driver's seat. At this point the sheriff decided that he should look a little more closely and found a sawed-off shotgun next to the driver's seat and another loaded handgun in the rear of the van. The sheriff rummaged through a pile of boxes and found an empty box for an Uzi submachine gun. This definitely got his attention. He asked the woman where the machine gun was, and she said that the boys had found the box in a dumpster behind a K-Mart and had just kept it. thinking it was "neat." At this point the sheriff determined that perhaps he needed to talk to Cole, who was still standing at the deputy's car near the motor home.

The sheriff approached Cole and asked him if he had an Uzi. Cole said he had a dummy of one that was not real and that this fake machine gun was still in the motor home. The sheriff told Cole, "Well, let's go take a look at it." By this time several other deputies had arrived and were all confused as to what was going on. One of them followed the sheriff and Cole to the motor home. As Cole started to enter the motor home in front of the sheriff, a newly arrived deputy grabbed him by the arm and said, "Maybe I better go first." All three entered the vehicle and started looking around. The whole time Harold was standing outside the large side window, and every time Cole would look out, Harold would raise the shotgun up toward him. This seemed to make Cole a bit uneasy, but then a shotgun pointed at most people would make them feel a bit nervous.

We could hear the sheriff ask Cole where that Uzi was located, and he answered, "Right here," and he started to reach toward the area between the driver's seat and engine compartment. The deputy, as he told me later, more as a reflex than conscious thought grabbed Cole's arm and said he would get it. He reached down and retrieved a black Uzi submachine gun. This was no dummy. It was a full automatic machine gun with a thirty-round magazine and a live round in the chamber, ready to go. At this point the sheriff made his final decision to hold these suspects at his jail until they could verify who they were. I told him I thought that was a good idea.

They brought Cole back out of the motor home and began to place him and one of the two women into the back of a patrol car. Harold blurted out, "Aren't you going to handcuff them?," and the chief deputy said that would not be necessary since they had a prisoner cage in the car. I then asked in a shocked manner, "Aren't you going to search them?" Again, the answer was that they did not need to since they had a prisoner cage. This was highly contrary to all the training and experience that the park service had afforded Harold and me. We felt very uncomfortable with this arrangement. As they started off on the way to the county court house, I told Harold that we better follow along, since the state magistrate might want to talk to us about why we had the vehicles stopped in the first place.

We followed close behind the deputy's car the entire eighteen-mile drive to town. Cole kept turning around in his seat, looking back at us, as if to see if we were still there. Every time he would turn around, Harold would point and shake his finger at him as if scolding a child. When we arrived at the jail, Harold and I stood in the background, but we assisted in herding Cole and the woman in the rear entrance. Cole kept his eyes on us the entire time. When the entourage finally arrived in the holding facility, the head jailer came out to meet us. He asked if the prisoner had been searched and one of the deputies said, "Sure." Both Harold and I immediately interrupted to correct this dangerously erroneous information. The other deputies looked on us with scorn. The jailer then decided that to be safe, he should search the prisoner himself. I could see the deputies' teeth almost fall out of their heads when the jailer pulled a loaded .25 automatic pistol from one of Cole's cowboy boots and a switchblade from the other. This revelation quickly explained why Cole had been looking back at us all the way to town. No doubt he was looking for an opportunity to escape.

The sheriff then asked if I would assist in searching the motor home and the van. By the time we finished, we had found numerous other loaded weapons hidden in both vehicles, two notary republic seals, blank birth certificates, seven sets of valid license plates for the van from four different states, numerous sets of drivers' licenses for Cole and the two women in a variety of names, and thousands of dollars in merchandise that had been stolen with bad checks, checking accounts, and blank checks from numerous banks in different states. And those were just a few of the items we found. Later, it was discovered that although Cole had rented the motor home in North Carolina, by falsifying documents he had taken it to Michigan and had obtained a legal title and registration for it. We also found that he was married to both women, who were sisters, and that the two young boys were his sons by each of the women.

The next day I was called by our dispatcher and was told that a Virginia State Police investigator wanted to see me. At the county courthouse, the investigator was in a jury room upstairs, sitting across a heavy wooden table from Cole. The investigator turned to me and said, "You must be Bytnar." Cole looked up at me with hatred in his eyes and spat out, "Yeah, I know who you are, and when I come back I'm going to get you." I have to admit, the way he said it sent a bit of a chill up my spine.

The next day the big headline in the Winston-Salem newspaper read, "Allegheny County Sheriff's Department Captures Interstate Criminal." There was no mention of the park service or of Harold and our participation whatsoever in the arrest. Then it dawned on me that no one from the sheriff's department had even thanked us for our assistance. I have to admit, that stung a bit.

A few weeks later, my supervisor and I were at a meeting with several police departments from Virginia. During lunch, one officer asked if we had heard of the big arrest that Allegheny County had made. Not catching on, I thought this referred to something that might have happened the night before. Then the officer began to recount how the sheriff's department had made this important arrest on Johnny Orville Cole, whom they had been after for years. The story was pretty exciting and made the sheriff's department look like a combination of Sherlock Holmes and Superman. The officer finished by saying that he hoped in his career he would get a chance to make a big arrest like that. All I could bring myself to do was laugh under my breath and finish my lunch.

As for Cole, several weeks after his arrest the state determined that because of his past escapes it would be better to have Cole in a more secure institution than the county jail. When they went to remove him from his cell, Cole had already removed the hinge pins from the cell door and was awaiting the right time to make his break. Once he got to the state pen Cole had some difficulties with a guard and ended up beating the guard pretty badly. Soon after that, Cole discovered religion and was released on parole after serving about two years. A couple years after Cole got out, Harold found a newspaper article from the eastern part of North Carolina in reference to warrants being issued for a Johnny Orville Cole for fraud involving passing bad checks. That is the last I ever heard of Johnny Orville Cole.

As to whether Cole will ever live up to his threat made years ago, I kind of doubt it. I believe he has since found plenty of other activities to occupy his time.

The Marshes of Wilkes

In 1983, I was working as a field ranger in the Bluffs district of the Blue Ridge Parkway in North Carolina. One busy Saturday afternoon, our supervisor, Dean Richardson, picked up some radio traffic from local agencies on his scanner. Apparently, the North Carolina Highway Patrol was in hot pursuit of a stolen car in Wilkes County. It sounded like they had just lost the suspects, who were reported as heading toward the Blue Ridge Parkway where there were two dirt roads where they could cross the park. Dean ordered me to one spot and ranger Harold Wood to the other.

We were sitting there for only a few minutes when, sure enough, the stolen vehicle with two occupants flew across the parkway right in front of Harold. He took off after them into Ashe County. I put the pedal to the metal and headed after them to provide backup. It soon became evident that as they had not stopped for the highway patrol, they were not going to stop for a park ranger. Harold continued after them, keeping a safe distance. I was several miles behind, trying to coordinate through our dispatcher with the county sheriff's department and the highway patrol.

The desperados turned off the main two-lane primary road onto a gravel secondary road after Harold had followed them for about ten miles. They must have figured out that the park ranger was not going to give up. A few minutes behind them, I pulled off on the same road.

As I came around a sharp hairpin switchback, I noticed out of the corner of my eye an old farm house just off the road. There was a man with no legs sitting in a wheelchair on the front porch, frantically waving his arms. As I passed him, trying to keep my car on the loose gravel road, Harold's excited voice blared out over the radio that the suspects' car had hit another vehicle, and that both of the suspects had bailed out of the car and attempted to run. No one was injured. Harold had the passenger in custody, but the driver had gotten away.

I turned my car around and went back to the house I had passed and jumped out of my car. The man in the wheelchair yelled to me, "He's up there." I turned to listen and could hear someone trying to run up the side of the mountain. He sounded like he was in a hurry, like a bull elephant busting his way through the brush. I grabbed my portable radio and started away from my car when a highway patrolman pulled up and told me to stop. I yelled over my shoulder, as I kept going, that the suspect was right above us and getting away. I was younger then, and my adrenalin was pumping like mad, so I kept going, still hearing the highway patrolman yelling at me.

As I crashed my way up the steep slope, I stopped periodically to listen for my prey. I could still hear him moving, and eventually I used this to zero in on his location. Finally I caught a glimpse of him through the trees, running uphill wearing a pair of jeans and no shirt. I started to gain some ground on him without his realizing that I was behind him. He was breathing hard and still making a racket in the loose ground cover, and tree limbs were smacking against him. Once I had gotten close enough and found some firm footing, I yelled, "Stop...police... You're under arrest."

He stopped turned and looked me in the eye and replied, "Fuck you," and took off running again. Now my adrenalin kicked into overdrive, and I was a bit mad. Here I had half killed myself, running up the mountainside, and this idiot was not going to immediately comply with my authority. Adrenalin can do strange things to your decision-making processes. I took off after him, determined not to let him go.

I challenged him a second time, and he still kept pumping up the slope. I gave it one last effort and caught up to him, attempting to grab his arm. He quickly turned and swung his right fist at my face. Luckily, he missed, because honestly I was too off balance to dodge the blow. He shook loose and started to bolt away. I dove at him out of desperation and was able to grab his lower legs, tackling him to the ground. He tried to roll away from me and kicked at me with his legs. I am still not sure how, maybe due to his exhaustion, but I was at length able to get him onto his stomach and handcuffed him with my knee in his back.

We both sat there for a moment, catching our breath. He rolled over, looked up at me, and said, "Nothing personal, man. You're just doing your job."

I breathlessly responded, "No, I think it's very personal. Why didn't you stop when I first yelled at you?"

He replied with a smile on his face, "I don't know."

I reached for my portable radio to report the capture only to discover it was gone. It must have fallen out of my belt case while I was running. Luckily, I had not lost anything else, such as my pistol. We began the long and much slower descent of the mountain, trying to retrace my steps to my vehicle, hoping to find the radio. I knew it would be like finding a needle in a haystack, but almost unbelievably, there the radio was, in the leaves about fifty yards above the road.

As we got closer to where I had started this crazy foot pursuit, I could see a large number of police vehicles from numerous agencies filling the road, and a gathering of officers were circled around a highway patrol sergeant, planning how to capture the fugitive. My prisoner and I slipped down the steep bank above my car and approached the group. Several turned toward us with disbelief on their faces. Recognition spread through the gathering, and suddenly two highway patrolmen pounced on us. They took the suspect away, threw him into the backseat of their vehicle, and whisked him away at high speed.

After the situation had settled down, ranger Dean Richardson and I spoke to the highway patrol sergeant and got more of the story. The person I had arrested was named Darryl Marsh. He had been convicted the week before for a third DUI (driving while under the influence) charge and had been given a week to get his affairs in order before reporting to jail. The night before, he and his friend, the passenger that Harold had arrested, had gotten drunk and were driving around, running people off the road. The highway patrol had gotten in a chase with them when Marsh had run the car off the road and into a ditch. Marsh and his buddy had bailed out of the car, escaping into the woods eluding capture. The car was towed and placed in a fenced impoundment lot. Marsh and his friend had gone to the impoundment lot during the day, climbed the fence, hot-wired the same car, drove it through the fence, and then another pursuit had ensued. Harold and I had gotten in on the tail end of that chase.

We later learned that Marsh, while waiting to appear before a state magistrate at the Wilkes County jail, had somehow been able to walk out of the building, jump into a county deputy's car that was sitting there unlocked and running, and then took off on another chase. Eventually, Marsh was caught again, and the police kept a better hold on him, this time getting him into a jail cell.

We also learned that Marsh's older brother was in prison for life for first degree murder. Apparently, the brother had gotten into an argument with their next door neighbor, then went home to get a shotgun and went back to blow the neighbor's head off. I then felt I knew what might have prompted Marsh to tell me that he was not going to take my catching him personally.

But that is not the end of the story of the Marshes of Wilkes.

About two weeks later, we received a report of a hit and run accident involving a car and bicycle. I was the first on the scene and found a crumpled and bent road bike and a badly shaken nineteen-year-old rider.

The biker told me that he was riding northbound on the Blue Ridge Parkway when he heard a car coming from behind him at what sounded like a high speed. He then heard tires squeal, and without thinking he threw himself from his bike, saving his life. The car ran over the bike and then took off, again squealing its tires. The cyclist did not get a good look at who was in the car, but miraculously he had the presence of mind to memorize the license plate.

I noted that there were almost two hundred feet of breaking skid marks leading to and over the bike, followed by almost two hundred feet of acceleration skid marks leading north away from the scene. Looking down at my notebook, where I had written the tag number, I suddenly had the strange sensation that the number was familiar. I ran a computer check on the tag number: damn if it did not come back as registered to the Marshes of Wilkes County, and it was the same tag number of the car Harold and I had chased two weeks before. It was like a déjà vu experience.

Once more help was on hand, I had to deal with the cyclist, who was hundreds of miles from home and now with no transportation or anyone that would come and pick him up. Evidently, he was on this trip very poorly equipped due to a conflict with his family. He had no money and no food and was now another victim of the Marshes of Wilkes.

I checked with the highway patrol, and they assured me that Darryl Marsh was still in jail and would be for a long time to come. Two highway patrolmen went to the Marsh home, way up in a holler, and only the tobacco-chewing mother of the family was at home. She said that the family did not have a car with that tag on it and told the patrolmen to get off her property. They returned later with a warrant and found the car, with the tags still on it, out behind the barn, covered with a tarp. The mother still claimed to know nothing about it. Her third and youngest son was also in custody and was a resident at a juvenile detention center near Asheville, North Carolina. After a little checking, we found that this third son, fourteen years old, was actually released on a weekend pass to spend time with his mother. Once we went back to her with this knowledge, the mother decided to confess to driving the car and hitting the cyclist and was so charged.

A week later I received a call from the juvenile detention officials in Asheville, wanting to know if I knew the whereabouts of young Mr. Marsh. Apparently, he had never returned to their facility from his weekend pass. I was not very surprised.

Mrs. Marsh's trial was several months later. She was obviously nervous, evidenced by the dark chewing-tobacco stains leaking from both corners of her mouth. She wanted to talk to the assistant U,S. attorney and me before the trial started. As we expected, she wanted to recant her confession and tell the whole story. According to Mrs. Marsh, she had gone to Asheville to pick up her youngest son from the juvenile detention center. She had been drinking on the way there, and both she and her son had continued to drink and take pills for twenty-four-plus hours straight to celebrate their reunion. They were on their way home, and her fourteen-year -old drunken criminal son was driving because Mrs. Marsh had passed out. It was then that they had hit the cyclist. They took the car home and attempted to hide it. Mrs. Marsh claimed to have no idea where her son was.

The charges were changed, and Mrs. Marsh was convicted of aiding and abetting and conspiracy. She went to jail for a month.

As far as I know, her youngest son never did turn up. I suspect he continued on his career to outdo his two older brothers' criminal deeds.

In 1986 I had transferred to another area, and Harold Wood sent me a newspaper article about Darryl Marsh. Marsh had been released from prison and shortly thereafter got involved in an argument at a convenience store in Wilkesboro, North Carolina, making threatening statements to a customer and an employee of the store. The clerk called the police, but they did not have anyone close by. She remembered that a man living across the street from the store was a guard at the local jail, so she went to his house for help. The jail guard went to the store, apparently calmed Marsh down, and got him to leave. Marsh then went to his car, took a tire iron from the trunk, went back into the store, and walked up behind the jail guard, hitting him in the back of the head, killing him instantly. The photo along with the newspaper story shows the victim being loaded into the back of an ambulance, while Daryl Marsh is standing by, watching and smoking a cigarette. The look on his face shows neither remorse nor a care in the world.

Once again, I remembered Darryl Mash telling me that he did not take my arresting him personally.

Stop in the Name of the Law

In 1982, I was working on the Blue Ridge Parkway in North Carolina, checking a section of boundary line. One of the many duties that fall to park rangers is to ensure that the park service's posted signs are still visible and to check possible encroachments or damage to park resources. This project had entailed climbing up and down the sides of several mountains, and by late afternoon I was confident that I would not have any trouble sleeping that night. I finally crawled and slid down the last slope and returned to my Jeep Cherokee and headed home, wondering what could be for supper. As I rounded a curve, there was a man right in front of me, violating the law by having the effrontery of hitchhiking in the park. I pulled over to explain that he could not solicit a ride on park property, and I learned that he was a Native American who was backpacking through the area and had to be at a local post office in two days to pick up a check from home. Being the big, tough guy ranger that I was (my wife always told friends that I would give my own mother a ticket), I offered to give him a ride to an area where he could camp legally for the night.

We were driving along, enjoying a conversation, when a motorcycle popped out from a side road and went straight through a stop sign without even slowing down and then onto the road in front of us. I hit my brakes and swerved to avoid hitting him. The motorcycle turned and went down the road in the opposite direction. I could not help but notice as he went by that the driver was not wearing a helmet, that he had no head light on as required by the state, and no license plate on the bike. All of these were violations in addition to running the stop sign. I felt like I had no choice but to stop this person and discuss his blatant disregard for the law and public safety.

I turned my vehicle around and went back down the road, attempting to catch up to the motorcycle. As I approached behind the bike, I turned on my emergency lights and blinked my headlights to get his attention. He did not make any effort to stop. I then sounded my siren. He turned around to look at me and kept on going, picking up speed. I stepped up my efforts to get his attention and sounded my siren again. He shifted the motorcycle's gears and took off like I was standing still. This action did not impress me, to say the least, and I sped up again. As my vehicle gained speed, I could also feel adrenalin starting to race through my body. One of the side effects of this physical condition is tunnel vision and a total focus on what is occurring in front of you.

As I finally got within sight of the motorcycle, he came upon a vehicle ahead of him and quickly passed it on a blind curve. As I approached the sedan full of family members with my siren blaring, the car pulled over out of my way. I then sped up again and caught up to the motorcycle. As I got closer on his tail, we approached a long, straight stretch of road. He slowed down, and I pulled up alongside of him. He signaled like he was going to stop, and I slowed down even more to get behind him. Suddenly, he turned, gave me the finger, and took off again at high speed. Now I was really getting angry with this guy, and I once again sped up close on him. As I got within about one hundred yards of the motorcycle, he turned off the park road onto a secondary state road, and I followed him down this narrow, paved lane.

While I was trying to figure out what this guy was up to and concentrating on driving a bit out of the routine, I was using the radio with one hand, trying to get other law enforcement officers to help me stop this motorcycle. What usually happens in these situations, though I am not sure why, is that everyone that has a radio suddenly wants to talk on it, and they always have questions to ask the person involved in the incident. People were asking repeatedly, "What is your location again?," which I was more than glad to answer, but I could not get a word in edgewise on the radio. Before I could even push the transmit button on the microphone, someone else would jump in to ask someone how close they were. This whole situation was further complicated by the problematic fact that events were moving in hyperdrive, spinning out of control, and I was not really sure exactly where I was at any specific moment. I knew what I had passed, but that might have been a half mile back or more. Thoughts start popping into my head: "What is my supervisor going to do if I wreck this vehicle?," and "What was that policy about pursuit driving outside the park?," and "Boy, is my wife going to kill me when she finds out I am late for supper again." It was probably all these factors that slowed my cerebral synapses, when suddenly it dawned on me that I still had the hitchhiker in the truck with me.

I quickly glanced over and noticed that he had been smart enough to buckle up his seat belt, and I asked him if he was alright. He looked over at me with a big grin on his face and said, "I'm fine. This is really great." At that point, I figured he could hang in there a little longer. I wondered then what my supervisor was going to think about this one.

We were following the motorcycle down the state road when his next maneuver was to cut off the road and through the front yard of a house. There was a man out in this yard pushing a lawn mower and looking down at the ground. The motorcycle zipped through the yard about thirty feet from him. and we zipped right behind him in the Jeep. I remember looking through my rearview mirror and seeing the man still pushing the lawn mower like nothing had happened. My impression was that either he had never even seen us go by or that this was a common occurrence in this neighborhood and hardly worth taking notice of.

At this point. the motorcycle went through the backyard

and directly into a standing field of corn. The corn was green and just about ready for harvest. I would have to say it was about as high as an elephant's eye. Before I had much time to even think about options, we were in the field, following right behind him with corn stalks banging around the Jeep. We came out onto a dirt road running through the middle of the field, still on the tail of the "vile violator." At about this stage in the chase, I got another call on the radio from the dispatcher, wanting a clearer idea of what state road I was on. I remember answering, "I don't see any state route signs out in this damn corn field." Under any circumstances, this was not appropriate radio usage. At this, my companion let out with a pretty good war whoop (it impressed me, anyway), and we sped down the dirt road.

After about a half mile we came to where the road ended at a small house. The motorcycle started around the house in a counterclockwise direction, with once again a ranger vehicle right on his tail. As we came around the other side of the house, an older woman was tending her flower garden under the windows. As the motorcycle went by, she was startled and stood up straight. As I went by, she jumped into the flower bed. We came right on around the house to where there was a six-foot-tall hedge. The motorcycle went right through it.

The adrenalin finally started to settle down in my body, and my brain started to function. This resulted in my realization that the Jeep I was driving might not make it through the hedge, and the little old lady I had just scared the heck out of would probably not appreciate a rather large hole in that same hedge. At that point I hit the brakes and drove around the hedge line. What we found on the other side was a spilled and abandoned motorcycle, with the operator nowhere to be seen.

Both the hitchhiker and I bailed out of the Jeep and made a quick dash around the area to look for the maniac that we had been pursuing. We had no luck and returned to the motorcycle. I did not want to leave the bike sitting there in case the owner came back for it. It was a pretty big bike, and there was no way

I could take it with us, so I reached over and ripped a bunch of wires off the ignition and coil. My companion and I then got back in the Jeep and headed out to the paved state road.

Once we arrived at the state road, we met a county deputy. After a few comments and laughs, he told me that based on my description he was pretty sure he knew who the culprit was. We then proceeded to follow the deputy to this person's residence at the end of a very long, dirt road, leading up into a dark hollow. There we learned that the fifteen-year-old boy that we were looking for had not returned home from his job in an orchard on the other side of the park. We also discovered that the only other person at home was his older brother, who had just gotten out of prison. Then to make the situation a little more complicated, it turned out that my immediate supervisor had been the one who put the older brother in prison. Needless to say, he was not at all pleased to see us.

I walked back down to my vehicle to wait for the boy's mother to come home, when off in the distance I heard the building whine of a motorcycle engine approaching on the dead-end dirt road. I thought to myself, "Nah, that couldn't be the same kid." About that time, around the curve, came the same boy on the same motorcycle. As soon as he saw me, he jumped off the still-moving bike and ran into the woods, down a steep bank. The uncontrolled motorcycle sped by me as I immediately took off after him on foot. I think I had a mental set that this guy was not going to get away from me. About that time a flash went by me, and the motorcyclist's brother passed me going down the slope. Before I knew what was happening, the brother tackled the fleeing suspect and started dragging him back up the hill. I met them at the road, and the brother just looked at me and said that he did not want to see his little brother get in as much trouble as he did with the park rangers.

After placing the elusive youth under arrest and in my vehicle, my supervisor contacted me on the radio and said that he would meet me out on the main road. Again I belatedly realized that I still had the hitchhiker with me. Quickly using my ranger savvy, I talked the deputy into giving my new-found partner a ride to the camping area. As he left, we shook hands, and he told me that this had been one of the most exciting experiences in his life.

I then drove out to the main road, where I met with my supervisor and another ranger. I gave them a quick, edited version of the big chase, and we took the violator off to jail.

The next morning, as I started up the Jeep, I noticed that the engine smelled like something was burning, so I took it to our mechanic to check it out. I was down in my office starting up the paperwork on this incident when the mechanic came and got me. He said that he had something that he wanted me to see. Now, one thing you do not want to do is anger the man who takes care of your vehicle. At this point he did not seem very pleased with me. As we walked to the shop, I had all kinds of visions of serious damage I had done to the Jeep and the grief that I was going to hear about it. We walked around to the front of the truck, and he dramatically (and painfully for me, I might add) opened the front hood. There before me, packed into every nook and cranny of the engine compartment, were stalks and ears of corn. This against the hot engine block was what I had smelled burning. The only comment that mechanic made was that I was lucky that it was not popcorn.

As for the motorcycle stunt driver, the federal magistrate found out that he had quit school at the age fourteen, and he was sentenced to three years probation. One of the conditions of the probation was that he had to go back to school and get his high school diploma. The boy stood there in the courtroom and begged to be sent to jail instead. I figured that the magistrate had been pretty smart in handing out this sentence. Of course, about a week later, I got a call from the high school principal, who was upset that this lad had been sent back to the classroom. The entire school system had been relieved that he had quit attempting to pursue a formal education the year before. This was just another example of how justice can never please everyone.

I never heard again from the hitchhiker, and most people,

including my supervisor at the time, were probably never aware of his participation in the caper until reading this narrative. I am sure he has a wild story about his ride with a crazy park ranger to tell his grandchildren.

Bears

One symbol that people often associate with park rangers is Smokey the Bear. The visiting public often asked how Smokey was doing (as well as Yogi and Boo Boo). Sometimes it is just innocent folks attempting to be humorous for their kids. When I gave presentations at schools on forest fire prevention and firefighting, children often asked about Smokey. Other times these comments came from those trying to be smart and turned rude. Just for the record, Smokey really belongs to the U.S. Forest Service, not my employer, the National Park Service, but even we had a hard time keeping that straight at times. I have to admit I have never seen Smokey the Bear while working, but I have had my share of bear experiences.

Bears are one of the species of wildlife that park visitors find most fascinating. When I was a kid, my family, like most other Americans in the 1950s and 1960s, watched all the Walt Disney movies and TV shows about bears in Yellowstone National Park and saw how cute and fun they were. Most children had teddy bears at some point in their lives. Although mine is long gone, my wife and I still treasure our now adult son's teddy bear, even though it is missing one ear, one eye, and its mouth. All these experiences contribute to the public's fascination with bears.

I will always remember when I first had the opportunity to work in an area inhabited by eastern black bears. I felt like I had finally reached a level of true rangerdom and was going to do real park ranger work—managing and protecting bears. Bears left alone in the park are generally no problem, but when you introduce the influence of man, things happen. I quickly built a long list of stories about the antics of bears.

There is a lot of development for housing just outside the Blue Ridge Parkway in Virginia, near Humpback Rocks. This entire area is prime bear habitat due to the availability of natural food sources and large rock areas in which to den up in winter. The development is reducing the amount of habitat available, so the bears look for other sources of food—trash cans, dumpsters, camp sites, vehicles, coolers; I think you get the picture. The Humpback Rocks Picnic Area has two large dumpsters near the entrance. Over time, I observed that the most popular food that the bears seemed to dumpster dive for was Kentucky Fried Chicken. They were real connoisseurs, preferring the original recipe over extra crispy. This deduction was not necessarily bound in scientific analysis, but if you were to enter this area early in the morning and see the trash that bears had removed from the dumpster, it more often than not contained a slightly abused Kentucky Fried Chicken (KFC) bucket.

We had one bear that had such a desire for KFC that we called him "the Colonel." We never did find the Parkway traveler who apparently met up with the Colonel late one night.

In 1986, one of the maintenance workers reported frantically over the radio that one of the restrooms at the Humpback Rocks Picnic Area had been vandalized. You could hear his indignation over the radio that someone would have the audacity to damage a facility that he dedicated himself to keeping neat and clean for the visiting public. I quickly responded to start an investigation, identify the culprits, and bring them to justice. Once I arrived at the scene and made some effort to calm the employee, I tried to make sense of his angry ranting. Unsuccessful at that, I entered the restroom. I found that the interior had been completely torn apart inside. The sinks were off the wall, and water was spouting everywhere. The stall walls had been torn down and the toilets ripped from their moorings. In the middle of the floor was a pile of trash, and in the center of this was a KFC bucket and a three-piece box, neither containing any chicken remains. I turned around and looked at the heavy wooden door that had to be pushed inward from the outside and found it covered with claw marks and bear paw prints. Using my Sherlock Holmesian deductive skills, I pieced together that "the Colonel" must have detected the succulent odors of leftover chicken in the restroom trash can. He had easily pushed the door open and feasted on the find. But when he decided it was time to go, he was unable to open the door again. He must have panicked and tore the place apart attempting to get out. The bear had obviously gotten out somehow, so we developed a theory.

This picnic area is not far from the city of Waynesboro, Virginia, and is frequented by local residents around the clock. At night, people who have been out partying and drinking often travel the Blue Ridge Parkway to avoid detection. So we imagined some person traveling home late at night and really needing to use a bathroom. He (it was the men's room) runs down the familiar trail from the parked vehicle and pushes the door open, only to be met face to face by the Colonel, who was far more intent on exiting the rest room then the other party was then interested in entering it. We never did receive a report from anyone of this happening, but it seemed the most logical and most entertaining solution we could develop for the Colonel's escape.

Not long after this event, two park maintenance crew members were sitting in their pickup truck eating lunch. They had been emptying litter cans before pulling into the Humpback Rocks Picnic Area for their meal break. They suddenly felt the back of the truck dip as if a weight had been placed on it. They assumed a visitor had walked up behind them and threw in another bag of trash. The driver got out to say hello and came face to face with the Colonel, going through the trash bags in the truck bed as if shopping. The maintenance worker jumped back into the truck, and the Colonel completed his inventory, gave a grunt, and wandered off.

This incident reinforced our decision that the Colonel needed to go. He was becoming too comfortable with being around people and their trash. We needed to trap him so he could be relocated to a safer and less populated area. We attempted numerous times to lure the Colonel into our culvert trap using all the standard and approved bear baits. Finally I brightened up and sent one of our seasonal park rangers to town for a three-piece KFC dinner (original recipe). We ate the biscuit and slaw and placed the rest, including the box, into the trap. The next morning we returned, and there was a very angry Colonel, no doubt reliving his experience of the rest room.

We transported him that day to a new location with better bear habitat. For some reason, as we were preparing to release him, I asked the ranger from that area if there was a Kentucky Fried Chicken restaurant near there. He said there was one about fifteen air miles away. For quite some time, whenever I thought of the Colonel, I had this image of a late night shift worker at the KFC and this bear standing at the drive-in window. I do not know where the Colonel may have traveled to, but I am sure he had a belly full of chicken.

Close Encounters of the Bear Kind

There was another bear I got to know up close and personal. We had a new ranger arrive to work in the district, and I was orienting her to the area, driving down the Blue Ridge Parkway. It was the middle of the day, and as we rounded a turn a bear ran across the road in front of my full-size SUV. Seeing a bear this time of year and day was unusual in that most were very shy and reclusive, since they were hunted with dogs in areas outside the park. We were both surprised and a bit excited by this sighting. I turned the vehicle around and drove back to see if we could get another look at the bear.

As we returned to the spot where the bear had crossed, we were both astonished to find the bear still standing there on the road shoulder. I had never seen a bear in this area hang around like this nor, as I thought about it, had I ever seen one in this particular area of the park. I was a bit puzzled by the situation. As we approached the bear in our vehicle, it sat there and stared at us. I beeped the horn and even turned on my siren, but the bear just sat there, looking at me.

I was concerned for the bear's safety. It was not uncommon for poachers from the local community to ride the park roads and shoot wildlife from their vehicles. I pulled up alongside of the bear, rolled down my window, leaned my head out, and tried to talk some sense into him, telling him he had better move off into the woods before someone came along and shot him. I noted as I looked down at him that he had slits in both his ears as if he had at one time had tags in them that had been ripped out.

I was still talking to the bear when, before I knew what was happening, he lunged up on his hind legs and placed his front paws on the door of my vehicle, stuck out his tongue, which seemed to be at least a foot long, and licked me right on my lips. I quickly leaned back into my vehicle, wiped my face with the back of my hand, and exclaimed "Yuck," or something like that.

When I looked back, the bear had both paws inside the edge of the open driver's side window, and he was pulling himself into the vehicle. At this point the new ranger had the good sense to bail out of the SUV. When I looked to my right, she was gone, and the passenger side door was wide open. As for me, running through my mind was how ridiculous this situation already was, and that I was not going to give up my vehicle to a bear.

Instinctively, or I maybe some would say stupidly, I reached out and slapped the bear on the nose. I believe that subconsciously I remembered from one of the Disney Davy Crockett movies that Davy had survived a bear attack by striking the bear in the nose. I must not have given as good a whack as old Davy, because the bear just opened his jaws and grabbed my wrist, biting through my watchband. Still, I was not ready to give up my vehicle, and besides, the bear's head was practically in my lap and it was too late to escape. So I hit the bear's paw that was now on the steering wheel with my fist, and he turned and bit me on my finger.

About this time my ex-passenger ranger realized I was not giving ground to the bear. She had to quickly choose between saving her new supervisor's neck and watching him be devoured by this denizen of the forest. In my opinion she chose wisely: She jumped back into the truck, grabbed my heavy metal flashlight from the center console, gave what sounded like a karate yell, and reached across me and bopped the bear a good one on the nose. The bear gave a yelp of surprise, backed out of the window, and ran down the bank to the edge of the woods, where he stopped and glared back at us.

Luckily, I was not seriously hurt. The bear had just nipped at me like a big dog would when playing rough. He did break the skin in one spot on my right hand. As I sat there, realizing what had just happened, I broke into laughter, thinking, "No one is going to believe this one."

The bear continued to sit there, glaring at us and not going into the woods. I finally drove farther down the road, turned around, and came back to find that the bear had at long last gone on down the mountain into the woods.

The next day I started to think about the bite breaking the skin I could not remember when I had last had a tetanus shot and decided I had better check in with our family physician. Along with my four-year-old son, Brian, I went to the local rural clinic. The doctor became extremely animated when I told my tale and immediately informed me that there had been numerous cases of rabies in the area among raccoons and skunks. He called the public health service office in the county seat. As I was sitting in his office I could hear my son down the hall in the waiting room, telling everyone about my adventure of the day before. Brian apparently had the entire audience wrapped around his finger as he relayed the tale.

The verdict from the public health service was that I needed to start rabies treatment immediately. I desperately attempted to call a good friend at the Great Smokey Mountains National Park, who was a wildlife biologist and expert on bears, to talk them out of it. Unfortunately, my friend was out of communications on a detail in Alaska. The only way to prevent my having to go through rabies shots would be to kill the bear so it could be checked for the disease. I packed my son up, and off we went to the local hospital.

My son, who was deathly afraid of needles, chose to again sit in the waiting area of the emergency room as I received my first five shots for rabies. As I exited, a bit sore and unsteady on my feet, Brian again had the crowd enraptured with the tale of his father's bear bite. At this point I realized there was no keeping this story under wraps.

As I laid in bed that night, finding it difficult to get comfortable after large gauge needles had been thrust into both arms and both buttocks (one cheek twice; they gave me a choice as to which one), little did I know that I would get to meet this same bear again.

Several days later, I was at home on my day off, still attempting to get comfortable, when the phone rang. It was one of the rangers I worked with calling to let me know that there had been another person bit by a bear a couple of miles from where I had my experience.

I was later able to interview the woman involved by phone at her home in North Carolina. She told me another interesting story. She and her family were traveling the Blue Ridge Parkway when they left to get gas in Buena Vista, Virginia. On the way back up the mountain toward the park, they saw a bear on the side of the road going through what appeared to be a pile of trash. They parked the car about fifty feet from the bear and exited the vehicle with cameras to get some pictures. Suddenly the bear lifted its head and started to walk toward them. The family became frightened and ran back to the car, quickly closing the widows and locking the doors. As they looked back toward the bear, they realized their mistake. They had left mom outside, She was slowed down, being on crutches with a cast on a broken foot. The bear stood up on his hind legs and wrapped his front legs around the woman's waist, giving her a bear hug. The bear then stuck out his tongue, which she described as being very long, and licked her on the lips (I know how she felt). She panicked and struck the bear with one of her crutches. The bear backed down, and she turned to make a stumbling run for the car, which still contained the rest of the family. As she moved off, the bear reached out and grabbed the rear of her good ankle in his jaws and bit down hard enough to just break the skin.

At that time a group of locals showed up in a pickup truck that the woman said had a large cage in the rear bed. As they approached the bear with a rope, he ran off into the woods.

She went to her doctor when she returned to North Carolina, and he did not feel it necessary for her to undergo rabies treatments.

Following this report, a bear hunt involving park rangers, U.S. Forest Service officers, and the state game commission ensued. Several hours into the hunt, one of the forest service officers came across a group of about ten locals on a back road. This group had a large, wire cage on the ground and a bear with a rope around its neck. They were attempting to pull the bear into the cage. Once they had the bear in the cage, the officer told the group that he was taking possession of the bear. The locals begged to differ and tried to drive away with the bear. It took the arrival of two park rangers, one of which exited his vehicle with his shotgun, to convince the group that they were not leaving with the bear.

The bear was then transported to the nearby U.S. Forest Service Work Center, where I arrived and IDed the bear as the same one that had bit me. They said they were going to have a line-up, but they could not get any other bears to volunteer. He had the two slit ears. which proved to be the indentifying factor. I also noted that he had a really long tongue, as I fed him raw hotdogs through the cage. It was quite obvious to everyone that this bear was accustomed to being around people.

Now I had to make a decision: to have the bear killed so it could be examined or to go through the rest of the rabies treatment. It was not hard for me to decide to stay with the treatment. After all, I had dedicated my life to protecting wildlife, and I could not bring myself to have the bear killed just because I got too close to it.

So the bear was taken to a state wildlife rehab center where it could be quarantined and observed for thirty days. At the end of that time, he was found to be healthy and eventually was taken to a new area where he could spend the rest of his days without fear of meeting another park ranger.

The biting bear and I shortly after his capture.

Two weeks after my bite incident my friend, the wildlife biologist from the Smokies, called me at my office. He was on a detail in Alaska dealing with bears in relation to clean-up operations following the Exxon Valdez oil spill. He was calling to let me know that he had requested through channels that I be detailed to work with him. I told him about my experience with the bear, and he informed me that there was no recorded history of a bear ever having rabies. I wished I had known this before. The request for the detail made it to my park superintendent's desk a day or so later. He said that there was no way he was going to send me to Alaska after being bitten by the bear because I was an embarrassment to the park and a laughing stock. So instead, he sent another district ranger who happened to be a golfing buddy of his and who incidentally knew absolutely nothing about bears or wildlife in general.

So missing out on the opportunity to go to Alaska was really the most painful result of the bear bite.

As a last post note: Several years after this incident an interagency investigation into illegal bear hunting in this general area revealed that this bear had most likely been one that was purchased in another state and illegally brought in to train bear-hunting dogs. The story was that this bear had escaped his captors and never been found. It is most likely the same one that bit both the woman from North Carolina and me. The bear had apparently been raised by humans and hand-fed most of his life. When I ran into him, he was not attempting to attack me. He was most likely just looking for a ride home.

Protecting Wildlife

It is the responsibility of the National Park Service and its rangers to not only protect the wildlife in the parks, but also the visitors who come by the millions. Preventing direct contact between wildlife and people is the toughest part of this job. Park visitors need to be aware of the consequences of their actions around wildlife and the impacts on the well-being of the animals and their own safety.

Here are some important tips to keep you and your family safe and to help the National Park Service preserve wildlife.

Remember that no matter how tame they may appear, all animals in parks are wild. They are not as they are often portrayed on television and in movies. A deer that approaches you is not looking to be your friend; it is looking for food. At any moment a wild animal can become aggressive to obtain that food. Keep your distance, enjoy the beauty of their presence, and then let them move on. Never approach a wild animal, and never offer it food.

Wild animals are biologically designed to eat the food that they find naturally in their habitat. Their day is centered on the constant search and browsing for food. Prepared human foods cannot be properly digested by most wildlife. The feeding of human food to deer is a good example. The whitetail deer has a digestive system similar to cows. They have multiple stomachs that the grasses, leaves, and acorns they normally eat travel through and process. They will be attracted to and eat human food because of the smell and ease of obtaining it off a picnic table or an outstretched hand. Once the food enters their digestive system, it cannot be broken down completely by the acids in their stomachs. This results in clogging the digestive system, and the deer slowly dies of starvation. When autopsied, the contents of the dead deers' stomachs show their cause of death was due from feeding by humans.

Other animals can become so conditioned by people feeding them that they lose their drive to forage for natural foods, which may alter their life cycles to a degree that it endangers their lives. On the Blue Ridge Parkway, there was a raccoon that became addicted to people feeding him at one of the overlooks. This raccoon, normally a nocturnal animal, altered its habits and started to hang out in the overlook during the day, begging for food. Visitors enjoyed the show and were more than glad to keep him filled up with potato chips and even jelly beans. We attempted on numerous occasions to chase the raccoon off during the day and also attempted to trap him so we could move him, but with no success. Within days, he would be back.

When winter came and snows began to blow, the number of visitors dropped, and the people willing to get out of their cars and see the raccoon plummeted. One visitor, fearing rabies, finally called in to report a sick raccoon at the overlook. When we checked the area, we found the same panhandling raccoon starving to death because he had lost his food source. We eventually were able to capture the raccoon and took it to a wildlife center. Unfortunately, his digestive system was so badly damaged that they were not able to save him.

No matter how fun it may seem, do not feed wildlife.

Of the most popular photo opportunities afforded in national parks are beautiful scenes of wildlife. Many people are so thrilled that they want photos of themselves or their children posed with the wildlife as if with their family pets. It is these photo ops that seem to result in the most injuries to people by wildlife. There are numerous stories of visitors being gored by bison in western parks because they got to close in trying to take a picture. I know of one instance in Shenandoah National Park and another recently told by a colleague out west where parents have put honey on a child's face or hands in attempt to get a bear to lick them. This is taking an incredible chance of bodily harm or even death. If a bear is offered food, it does not know to stop once you have had your fun.

Do not approach, crowd, or attempt to lure wildlife. Give them their space, back away, and let them go on their way. Remember, you are a visitor in their home, and show them the respect they deserve since you are their guest.

Poachers

An important facet of a national park ranger's duty is the protection of natural and cultural resources within a park. One of the most highly visible of these resources is the wildlife. Animals benefiting from residing in a protected area are not often pursued or hunted and so become conditioned to the presence of humans. This produces an incredible opportunity for park visitors to view wildlife in its natural habitat, but it also sets those animals up as easy pickings for illegal hunters who want to take the best of a species from the American citizenry. Criminals illegally take many species of wildlife from our national parks for profit and in some cases merely for bragging rights and trophies. It is an ongoing challenge for park rangers to prevent this slaughter in the parks.

When demand exists and money is to be made, it is amazing what suddenly has value. One of the pressures placed on resources within our national parks is the international market for wildlife and plants. This trade has elements similar to the stolen car business, where a vehicle is stolen and then broken down for parts and sold in different locations and jurisdictions. The demand from East Asian cultures for black bear gall bladders is just one example of this trade in illegal wildlife. Bears are broken down for their galls, paws, claws, and teeth. Then of course, there are the hides and meat. Whitetail deer that are in velvet growing their annual antlers are killed and the antlers sold, leaving the rest of the carcass behind to rot.

In Korea and China, the dried gall bladder of a black bear is valuable as a folk medicine for the treatment of blood disorders. As an example, at one time galls were bought into this country from illegal wildlife poachers (and in some instances, legally from hunters) for anywhere from sixty to ninety dollars apiece. By the time that same gall was dried and placed on the market in Korea, the price increased to as much as three thousand dollars. This market is so strong in Asia that in many regions bears have become extinct, resulting in the search for sources in other parts of the world. In the mid-1990s undercover agents from the Virginia Department of Game and Inland Fisheries bought more than sixty illegal gall bladders in the Shenandoah Valley from one individual. That meant that sixty bears had been killed and most likely illegally for these galls. It has been common in the past to find bear carcasses with the gall bladder removed and the rest of the bear left to rot.

This marketing of wildlife even spreads to other species such as deer, turkey, salamanders, and even snakes. Plants are also taken for monetary profit.

A mythical misconception exists that poachers are often-times akin to Robin Hood and just trying to feed their families. In thirty-two years I have never met a person like that. The poachers I dealt with were involved in other criminal activities such as drugs, burglary, embezzlement, assaults, and murder and used money generated by this additional illegal activity to support their habits and other criminal pursuits. Another common thread was to kill wildlife for the bragging rights or to improve their status amongst their peers.

I first experienced poachers for commercial profit while stationed at Fredericksburg and Spotsylvania National Military Park in Virginia. There was an active market for deer meat in a number of Washington, D.C., restaurants that specialized in gourmet meals featuring wild meat. During this period of the mid-1970s, there was even a minor political scandal when it was found that the sitting secretary of the interior frequented such a restaurant and regularly enjoyed his favorite dish that included rattlesnake. Upon investigation by agents from the U.S. Fish and Wildlife Service, it was found that the species of snakes served were on the endangered species list and had been taken illegally and sold to the restaurant.

At Fredericksburg and Spotsylvania National Military Park, our problem was the killing of whitetail deer within the park by a technique commonly called "spotlighting." This entails driving around in a vehicle just after dark when the deer are most active and feeding on the preferred open grass fields and road shoulders. The poacher then shines a spotlight or turns the headlights of their vehicle onto the deer. The deer's natural instinct is to freeze and stand still, making use of its coloring to blend in with its surroundings. They believe that they are invisible to the possible predator. The deer's eyes reflect the light back to the hunter as amber orbs, further highlighting the location of the deer. The poacher merely has to step from the vehicle and shoot a very short distance at a lighted target to kill the deer. It is literally like shooting fish in a barrel. Once the deer see movement or hear a loud sound, they will run off. Some more advanced poachers will use small caliber rifles or even silencers so they can shoot more than one deer with each stop.

One night I was working solo, with no one else to monitor my radio transmissions should I call for help. This was standard operating procedure at that time. I was patrolling the Wilderness Battlefield when I drove to an area known as the Widow Tapp Field. I could see from down the road that there were bright lights flashing around in the night sky. As I got closer, I turned off my headlights and slowed my patrol car to a crawl. I could see a pickup truck in the gravel vehicle pull-off and an arm hanging out of the driver's side window with a portable spotlight directed into the field. I pulled in behind the pickup. The occupants were distracted, looking into the lit-up field that contained what looked like a large number of deer with their eyes glowing like small neon signs. I put my car in park (I mention this because at times like this, when adrenalin is pumping and you are going into a possibly dangerous situation, tunnel vision takes over, and one can forget about putting the car in park) and turned on my emergency lights. Immediately, the spotlight went out, and I could see that there were three heads in the pickup. No one turned to look at me. They just sat there, frozen.

I slid out of my car and called for the driver to step out of the vehicle. The only reaction I could see was what appeared to be a discussion amongst the occupants and some movement between the two passengers. Again I ordered the driver out of the truck. After several seconds, there was still no reaction. My adrenalin was starting to pump even harder, and the threat radar in my head was buzzing. What were these guys planning?

I stood there in what was starting to look like a standoff. I thought that either they were hoping I would just leave or perhaps they wanted me to walk up to the truck and expose myself. I knew I had stepped into it and did not have any way to call for help. After what seemed like an eternity but was in reality no more than three minutes, I reached back into my car and pulled out my .12 gauge pump shotgun. I moved forward just enough so that the shotgun was illuminated by the light bar on the roof of my car and I racked a round into the chamber. The sound of a shotgun racked or loaded is a distinctive and loud sound that can be accentuated by darkness and fear. As the shotgun shell settled into the chamber I commanded again, "Driver exit the vehicle." The driver came out so fast he tripped over his own feet, almost falling to the ground. Even I was a bit surprised by this sudden urgency of compliance. I was able to get all three of them out of the truck and spread eagle on the ground. It was then safe for me to go to their vehicle and remove the two loaded rifles they had been trying to hide between their legs.

In 1982, I was working on the Blue Ridge Parkway in North Carolina when my supervisor and I ran into another group of spotlighters. We were working late at night during hunting season, conducting a surveillance of an area frequented by feeding deer and poachers. We had watched several vehicles move through the area but had not seen any suspicious activity, and we were about to call it quits when we observed a vehicle moving unusually slowly toward our position. In the dark, we could just barely make out what appeared to be a weak light flashing out from the side of the car. It was so indistinct that we had to question each other as to what we had seen. Suddenly, the vehicle pulled off the road, shined its headlights through an open area, turned around, and then headed off in the opposite direction. We decided we had enough reasonable suspicion to stop the vehicle and see what they were up to.

We finally got the car stopped about two miles up the road. The vehicle was a large, older model sedan with what looked like three people in the front seat. My boss approached the driver's side of the suspicious car. and I walked up on the passenger side. I noticed as I gave the car a quick glimpse that there was something smeared over the rear license plate and chrome bumper. In the backseat of the car was a woman laying across the seat as if asleep, and three people were in the front seat. On the front floorboard was a cheap, plastic two-cell flashlight. This must have been the source of dim light we had seen being shined from the car into the fields as they passed. My boss was asking for some identification from the driver when I stepped back to take a closer look at the trunk area. Upon closer examination, I found what now looked like blood and deer hair smeared all over the rear of the car. I reached down to touch the bumper and found the blood to be still wet and fresh. I stepped forward again and shined my light around the interior of the car, not seeing any obvious signs of weapons.

I called my supervisor back to the rear of the car and showed him the blood. We then commanded the occupants to exit their vehicle one at a time, and we stepped to the front of the car so we could see them in the headlights. The woman in the backseat was unresponsive. and the others said she was a hard sleeper and had not been feeling well. At first they suggested and then insisted that we leave her alone. I had finally had enough, opened the backdoor, and tapped her on the bottom of the foot with my flashlight. She stirred and mumbled but did not get up, even after being commanded to do so. I then grabbed her by the ankle and began to pull her from the vehicle, and she popped up and started to cuss. We immediately noticed that she had been lying on top of two loaded rifles. Her subterfuge was an attempt to hide them from us. At this point, they knew the game was up, and we handcuffed and search all four suspects.

Upon opening the trunk we found a mess of blood, gore, and hair, all of which were later identified as coming from deer. Apparently, they had shot several deer already that night and had unloaded them and come back for more when we happened upon them.

A few days later, I got a telephone call from an Alcohol Tobacco and Firearms (ATF) special agent asking me about the group we had arrested. He wanted to know how we had managed to arrest them without having to shoot them. Apparently, the driver had been in at least two shootouts with ATF and FBI agents during previous arrests. The only reason I could come up with was that they thought we were just some local yokels that they could snow and get away with their poaching. By the time we had found proof of what they were up to, it was too late for them to try to resist. The driver ended up having to go back to prison for probation and firearms possession violations and served twelve years. One of the arrested suspects later admitted that they had been killing up to seven deer a night and selling the meat to a local distributer for restaurants. They were getting twenty dollars per deer they brought in. This information was turned over to the state of North Carolina for the prosecution of the distributer.

You never knew how you would find or catch a poacher. Sometimes poetic justice would lend a hand in the apprehension.

One night in 1995, I received a call at home from a woman reporting that her son had been involved in a motor vehicle crash on the Blue Ridge Parkway near Waynesboro, Virginia. I asked if he was still at the scene and she said, "No, he is here at the house, but the car is still up there." I instructed her to bring her son back to the scene and told her that I would meet them there. At the scene, I found a Ford Pinto flipped over on its roof with the rear hatchback open. I noticed that there was a lot of blood smeared on the glass window and interior of the rear storage compartment. My first impression was that the driver and any other occupants must have been injured and crawled out the back of the car that had its front hood hanging precariously over the mountain edge. When the mother returned with her son. I noticed that he did not have any obvious bleeding or head wounds, which often result in lots of blood loss.

His story was that he and a buddy were driving down the road when a deer ran out in front of them, causing him to swerve and run off the road. When I asked where the friend was, I was informed that he had gone home. I asked if he had any injuries, and the driver said, "No, he was okay." The young man then started to complain about his head hurting, and it began to sleet and snow. I told the mother to take her son to the local hospital and that I would meet them later.

While waiting for a wrecker to arrive and remove the car, I had time to more closely examine the blood in the car. What I found was that the blood also contained hundreds of short brown and white hairs that looked like deer fur. Flashing my light around on the ground, I found what appeared to be drag marks with blood leading around the car and down the steep mountain slope. Following the trail, I eventually found the carcass of a dead female whitetail deer that appeared to have been shot. I returned up the now snow- and ice-slicked slope to the road where I met the wrecker operator. By the time the car was removed, the sun was starting to spread its yellow light down the mountainside before me. As I looked down at the deer I had found, I thought I saw more brown fur in the brush below it. I crawled carefully down the now even more precarious slope and found another deer carcass. As I stood there scanning the scene, I looked to my left and found a third deer carcass.

As I drove toward the hospital to meet with the mother and driver, I stopped at several locations where I knew deer frequented at night. In the Humpback Gap Parking Area I found what appeared to be blood pooled on the pavement under the still transparent layer of snow. Nearby I found more blood and deer hair on a split rail fence where it appeared that a shot deer was dragged across from the field beyond to the parking lot.

At first, the driver denied any knowledge of any deer being in his car when it crashed. He was eighteen years old and therefore legally an adult. I was able with some difficulty explain to his mother that I could question him without her being present and was able to get her to leave the examination room. Once she was gone and the young man was faced with the facts I had gathered, he confessed that he and his buddy had spotlighted and killed three deer in the park that night. They were on their way to a friend's house to unload the deer when, as he had stated earlier, a deer ran in front of them, causing him to wreck his car. They had then dragged the deer carcasses out of the car and down the mountainside to hide them. His plan was to call a state trooper to investigate the accident since he did not think they would be interested in or pay any attention to the deer. It was his mother who thwarted his plans by reporting it to the park service.

To add further insult to injury for these two geniuses of crime, following their initial appearances in federal court they were released on bond with numerous conditions of keeping their noses clean. When they reported for their court dates, the U.S. probation officer assigned to their case required them to take a drug screen. Both defendants showed positive for marijuana and cocaine. They were immediately taken into custody by the U.S. marshals service and stayed in jail for over a month until their trial was rescheduled. Once convicted of numerous violations related to the deer and bond violations, they both served an additional six months in jail, forfeited several firearms that were seized during searches of their residences, and were assessed large fines.

The Mountain Slide

I was working in the Doughton Park area of the Blue Ridge Parkway during hunting season in 1982 when a fall and slide down a mountain resulted in the capture of two poachers illegally hunting on park service lands. Ranger Harold Wood and I had been out since well before dawn, patrolling for hunters that had crossed the line onto national park service lands where such activities were prohibited.

It had been a long and unproductive morning. It appeared that either everyone was obeying the law or we had not been in the right place at the right time to catch any violators. I told Harold that my wife was expecting me home for lunch and invited him to come along. He wanted to hike down the Flat Rock Ridge Trail to make sure no one had slipped from the adjoining Thurmond Chatham Game Lands into the park. I drove a half mile away to our house, where my wife greeted me with homemade potato soup and cheese bread, which tasted appropriately delicious on a cold, late fall morning.

I was about halfway through my second bowl when the park radio began to crackle, and I could barely hear what sounded like someone whispering over the air waves. I got up from the table in the kitchen and walked into the living room where the radio was mounted on a bookcase. As I strained my ears to listen, I could just make out that it was Harold sounding like he was trying to talk quietly on the radio. His voice's resonance was strange, and I realized it was due to it being raised a few octaves higher than normal. This meant something big was going on because Harold was a pretty level-headed guy.

"402, 403."

"This is 402," I responded, with anticipation in my voice to learn what Harold was into now.

A soft, whispered voice came back, "I'm out on the Flat Rock Ridge Trail about a mile from the parkway and have two guys with rifles below me."

"Are they in the park? I mean, are they on the park service side of the ridge?"

"Yeah, yeah, they are right below me talking. They are way inside the park."

"Okay, do you want me to meet you on the trail?" I asked.

"No, they are moving down the drainage into the park," Harold said. "So drive around to the bottom of Basin Cove, and I will follow them out through there."

"10-4, I'll see you down there." I grabbed another slice of warm cheese bread and headed out the door, not taking the time to explain to my wife where I was disappearing to this time. As I drove the twenty-two miles around on state roads to the base of the hollow Harold was trailing the poachers through, I was unable to contact him by radio. With our ancient portable radios, this did not worry me too much, since it was common to lose radio contact once you dropped below any of the ridges in that area. I finally arrived at the foot of Basin Cove directly below Harold's last reported position. I parked my car at the Grassy Gap Fire Road gate and waited for him. Finally, I heard him call on the radio.

"402, 403. I am coming out to the Fire Road. I have one of the guys in custody. The other ran from me and wouldn't stop."

"I'm down here at the gate now." I replied. "I will stand by for you and keep my eyes open for the other suspect."

About fifteen minutes later I saw Harold leading a man dressed in camouflage down the fire road toward me. Harold was carrying a rifle with a large scope, and I noticed that he looked a bit more disheveled then he had the last time I had seen him. We questioned the suspect, who insisted that he had been hunting alone and did not know he was in the park. Harold had gotten his driver's and hunting licenses and identified him as Robert Queensberry. He kept denying that he had been hunting with anyone else. When Harold confronted him with the fact that he had seen him talking with another hunter who had run from him, he said that it had been some guy he had just met in the woods. We figured we were not going to get any further information out of Queensberry, so Harold issued him violation notices for hunting in the park, and we placed him in the back of my patrol car.

Harold and I could now talk in private and compare notes on our questioning. We both agreed that Mr. Queensberry was being less than honest with us. Being quite impressed, I asked Harold how he had caught the poacher. He said that not long after calling me on the radio, he was attempting to work his way down the ridge toward the two suspects when a rock slid out from under his foot. He fell on his butt, his feet flying out from under him, and slid down the steep mountain side for almost seventy-five yards, bumped off a downed and rotted tree, went airborne, and landed on his feet almost in the middle of the two men. They had both stared at this apparition of a park ranger with complete disbelief, their mouths agape, when Harold shouted, most likely in his high octave voice of excitement, "Park ranger, halt, you are surrounded!" Robert Queensberry just stood there as if his feet were set in concrete. The second suspect turned and ran. Harold yelled for him to stop, but he kept crashing his way through the dense underbrush and rhododendron. This manner of approach to his suspects explained Harold's unusually disheveled appearance.

We asked Queensberry where his car was parked, and he directed us up a road onto the Thurmond Chatham Game Lands. With my patrol car scraping bottom, we worked our way up the narrow, rough dirt and rock track to a widening where two vehicles were parked, a jeep and a pickup truck. We asked Queensberry who the other car belonged to, and he said he did not know. He was agitated and angry now, since he found out we were keeping his rifle as evidence and there was another week left of deer season. He also became a bit surly now that he found out he merely had a court date assigned and was not going directly to jail. As he was starting to load himself into his pickup, I started to wonder who the other car belonged to. I was able to contact our dispatcher on my car radio and learned that the jeep was registered to a Michael Queensberry from the same small North Carolina town as Robert. We asked him once again who he had been hunting with and who owned the other vehicle. He replied, "I have no idea whose jeep that is, and I was hunting alone."

"So where is your brother?" Harold asked.

Queensberry's face went pale, losing all color. His eyes quickly diverted away from us. "I don't know. Why do you ask?"

"Because this here jeep is registered to him, that's why," Harold quickly answered.

Queensberry looked like all the air had been let out of his body. He dropped his shoulders, his head dropped, and after a moment or two of silence he responded, "Yeah, okay, my brother was hunting with me. We did not see any deer all morning on the state game lands so we thought we would see what we could find in the park."

"Where is he now?"

"I don't know, he ran from you and he has not shown up here I guess. He might be lost."

"Why didn't you run like your brother?"

"When you came out of nowhere, it scared the shit out of me, and I froze. When I saw my brother take off, I thought about running but then remembered my bad knee and just figured I was caught."

Now the question became how to locate the brother. The obvious professional answer was that we back off, watch his jeep, and wait in stealth for him to return. But by this point Harold and I had been working for twelve hours. I had eaten lunch, but Harold had gone all day without food. So in a desperate ploy I went back to my car and switched my radio from transmit to the public address system. Picking up the microphone I called out to the wilds, "800, 402." I waited a moment and repeated, "800, 402."

After another pause I then spoke into the microphone in a deeper, slower, and more southern voice, "402, this is 800."

"800, 403 and I are located on the Thurmond Chatham Game Lands road and need a wrecker to tow a Jeep CJ to be impounded."

Back in the false voice, "402, I copy that you need a wrecker at Thurmond Chatham. Stand by." I called out to Harold and Queensberry, "Dispatch is calling a wrecker. It should be here soon."

Queensberry looked worried. "What do you need a wrecker for?"

Harold responded, "We are going to impound your brother's truck as evidence."

Queensberry was even more shaken now.

From my car over the PA you could hear my magnified, dramatic voice again reverberating off the steep, wooded walls of the hollow, "402, 800. We have that wrecker on the way. It should be there in about twenty minutes."

"Thanks 800. We are standing by."

After about ten minutes nothing stirred, nothing moved around us. We could hear the light breeze work its way through the huge hemlocks that surrounded us. But there was still no sign of Michael Queensberry.

Suddenly, Harold sprung to his feet. "I've had enough of this." He strode over to my car and grabbed the PA microphone. "Hey, Mickey. We know you're up there somewhere. We are going to tow your car out of here, and you are going to have a long walk home if you don't come out."

Within what seemed like less than a minute, we observed a camouflaged man about the same size and stature as our captured poacher nonchalantly walking down the road toward us, a rifle slung over his shoulder. It was Michael Queensberry, who had apparently been within a hundred yards of us the entire time. We had just barely beaten him to his vehicle, cutting him off. He completely denied having been in the park and claimed not to know that his brother had been hunting that day. Unfortunately for him, Harold could identify both of them, and Robert Queensberry had already spilled the beans.

We confiscated another rifle and issued numerous violation notices to another disappointed hunter and released them with a date to appear in court.

When the court date arrived in Asheville, North Carolina, both brothers were found guilty of hunting on national park service lands and of possession of loaded firearms. Michael got an additional conviction for failure to obey a lawful order after running from Harold. Both received stiff fines and lost permanent possession of their rifles and other hunting gear we had confiscated as evidence. In addition, they both received a one-year period of supervised probation and were banned from all federal property. They avoided an active jail sentence since they both had no previous record.

I will always remember Harold's slide down that mountainside. If he had not fallen, we very likely would never have had the opportunity to use our less than orthodox operating procedures to capture this duo of sibling violators.

Plants

I often believe that every resource within a national park has a value attached and is threatened by theft or what we refer to as poaching. Plants are no exception. There are thriving big money markets for plants that are found in our parks. These markets include landscaping, ornamental flower arrainging, food sources, religious, and medicinal and folk remedies. Many rare and highly desirable plants are only found in national parks, and they may have added monetary value if taken from a park because of the guarantee that the plant grew in a natural environment. In national parks there are no man-made chemical fertilizers or pesticides used to aid in growth and development of the plant. Criminals think of it as free organic crops propagated for their profit.

The economic state of our country also affects the theft of plants and poaching of other resources. Generally, when the economy declines and jobs begin to become scarce, there is a sharp increase in the number of people taking plants for profit.

Several years ago a park ranger was driving on the Blue Ridge Parkway in Virginia when she passed an overlook with a parked, large, older model sedan that appeared to be unattended. Knowing there was no trail that left from this parking area, she slowed as she drove past and observed several people farther off in the woods looking at the ground. The ranger knew that this area was prime habitat for several species of plants desirable to thieves. Her suspicions raised, she parked her car out of sight and walked back toward the sedan. As she approached, one of the individuals exited the woods, approached the car, and put what looked like a small item in the trunk. The ranger approached this gentleman and noticed that he had dirt on his hands and knees. When questioned, he informed her that they were just looking around and denied that they were digging up any plants. The ranger was finally able to persuade the gentleman to give her permission to open the trunk. What she saw surprised her.

Neatly placed in cardboard boxes were more than fifty freshly dug plants of various species. The majority were wildflower plants such as trillium, jack in the pulpit, several orchids, irises, and lady slippers. There were also digging tools and more containers that could be used to hold plants. Once the ranger had evidence that a crime had been committed, a more complete search of the vehicle was made. In the glove box was a handwritten list of native plants, noting both the common and scientific names. This list was on stationary from a national hotel chain. A rumpled and creased edition of the Blue Ridge Parkway's folding map, which had not been printed for over twenty years, was also found with handwritten notations of locations for plants in great detail by species, which side of the road, and how far from the road they would be found. Two of the individuals with the car were from New York City, and the other two were a couple from Germany. The two Americans were apparently assisting the Germans in collecting plants to take home for either sale or placement in their personal garden in Europe. We never learned more specific details, since once released by the court none of them returned for their scheduled trial.

What was discovered in this case was an example of the international trade in native plants of the Southern Appalachians. There was no telling how many plants had been taken through the years by this one obviously organized group.

Another plant that is found growing wild in the Southern

Appalachians is the ginseng. This plant is valuable for its root, which is used in many energy-inducing and blood-thinning remedies. It is extremely valuable in Asian markets, where the wild ginseng has become all but extinct from over harvest. In American pharmacies and even television commercials, you will find pills and drinks that are advertised to contain ginseng.

Since it is the root of the plant that is used in these concoctions, the entire plant is taken, leaving no replacement for the next season. Old-time "Sangers," as they are know in the mountains of the South, will pinch the red berries during digging time to spread the seed for the next growing season. They will guard the knowledge of these locations as their secret patches and return year after year, harvesting the mature plants. Today's quick-profit-oriented ginseng hunters in most cases do not take the time to make such efforts. They find the plants, dig the roots, and are gone. The cash incentive can be high. In 2007 one pound of dried ginseng roots could be sold for a thousand dollars.

There are places where ginseng can be dug legally on U.S. Forest Service and state lands with permits that determine limits during established seasons similar to hunting seasons for game. Individuals are still lured by greed to venture into protected areas such as national parks for what they consider easy pickings. Researchers are finding a decrease in the population of ginseng in the mountains of the south. Using less scientific methods, there are other indicators.

On the Blue Ridge Parkway, there seemed to be a pattern of observing and apprehending ginseng hunters from West Virginia coming to Virginia. When interviewed, a common theme among these violators was that they could not find ginseng in West Virginia anymore, causing them to venture across state lines to make a profit.

Another indication of the decline of populations of this plant is that park rangers are reporting seeing fewer signs of the plant while patroling backcountry trails and boundaries. I know from my personal experience that areas where I could

find significant and healthy populations of ginseng were disappearing over the years. Locations where we would take new
employees to see the plants so they could identify them were
gone. In two instances we found evidence of the plants being
dug up by perpetrators within days of our arrival at the site.

Another common plant that is taken from the parks is
galax. Galax plants produce a rich and lush high-elevation forest ground cover with large, flat, glossy green leaves that can
be four to five inches across. These leaves have a long shelf life
once cut that makes them popular in the florist industry for
flower arrangements. The gathering of the leaves for sale to florist distribution warehouses has been a source of money in the
region for decades.

When I worked on the Blue Ridge Parkway in North Carolina during the early 1980s, most people collecting galax were
local residents attempting to make a little extra money. In fact,
the collecting of galax leaves was considered by the managers
of the Blue Ridge Parkway as a traditional mountain activity,
and they did not want park rangers enforcing the regulations
to prevent it. I was berated by my supervisor when I caught
two locals dragging four large burlap sacks of leaves from the
woods to their car. I had issued them violation notices for possession of native plant material in the park and confiscated the
sacks stuffed full with several thousand galax leaves. By the
coming of the new century the complexion of this business
took a drastic change, and so did the attitude of park service
managers.

Once again biologists and researchers started to observe a
drastic decrease in galax plant populations at higher elevations
along the Blue Ridge Parkway. Areas that in previous years had
been carpeted with galax were found to be barren. When park
rangers with experience in tracking were called in, they found
trails worn through these areas that rivaled developed high-
ways. It became obvious that the decline in plants was due to
heavy illegal harvesting as had never been seen before. Even on
adjoining lands managed by the U.S. Forest Service, the decline
in galax populations resulted in the closing of areas previously

open for its collection and restrictions on the times that galax could be collected in other locations.

Further investigation revealed that scores of illegal immigrants, mostly from Mexico, were being brought into the area specifically to harvest galax leaves for the floral industry. Each individual undocumented alien could make up to two hundred dollars a day pulling and cutting galax leaves, then packing them into large duffle bags. The leaves are packed in bundles of twenty-five and are held together with twisty ties. The duffle bag full of leaves is then sold to florist supply warehouses for anywhere from one cent to five cents per leaf. Full duffle bags confiscated during arrests of several of these plant poachers contained from two to three thousand leaves. During one surveillance operation at least a dozen men were observed leaving the park, each carrying at least one overstuffed duffle bag. That adds up to, in one day, in that one specific area, a minimum of 24,000 galax leaves taken illegally from the Blue Ridge Parkway.

An additional part of this business is the drivers hired to drop off poachers early in the morning and then pick them up late at night. Each plant poacher pays the driver twenty-five dollars a day. Most of these drivers, who are local residents, can make between two hundred and two-hundred fifty dollars a day, depending on how large a vehicle they have and how many people they can fit in it.

These are only three examples of plant theft that is occurring within our national parks. With our sagging economy, the competition for plants of value will only increase, placing more pressure on the resources of our parks. This situation is well beyond the occasional individual picking a few flowers to take home to grace their table. These people are commercially motivated and in some cases very organized criminals, stealing the legacy of the American people. Part of the reason that these plants have become so valuable is that their near relatives have all but disappeared in other parts of the world where the market still exists for their sale. If left unchecked, our own nation will eventually become devoid of these same native plants. Preventing plant theft is a time-consuming job that involves team work between biologists, park rangers, and the public.

These plants are located in habitats that are also threatened by environmental enemies. Trees that provide the shade and moisture for many of these ground plants are being stressed and in many instances eventually killed by such pests as the fungus dogwood anthracnose, oak leaves are eaten by gypsy moths, and hemlocks are being killed at an alarming rate by wooly adelgids. These dying native plants and trees are then being replaced by exotics such as kudzu, multi-flora rose, garlic mustard, tree of heaven, and many more. Declining air quality in many regions is also producing stress on these same trees, making plant survival and control of pest infestations even more difficult. As the fragile habitat shrinks and theft increases, the future of native plants in many national parks becomes questionable.

Hopefully, awareness of the threats to these resources will enlist more eyes in the parks tuned to looking for plant thieves and the reporting of their activities. If park rangers know the locations where thefts are occurring, they are better able to concentrate their efforts and make an impact through arrests that result in federal court convictions.

So the next time you are out in a park, whether a national, state, or local park, with your family on a hike, and you see people digging, people with digging tools, people acting furtive with dirt on their hands and clothes, or people loading plants in a vehicle, contact someone from that park and pass the information on. Who knows, you may become an important initial starting point in stopping an international criminal operation.

Which Way to Lynchburg?

It was a muggy, summer night, and I was patrolling from Cumberland Knob to Doughton Park on the Blue Ridge Parkway in North Carolina. when my headlights picked out what looked like a large car off the right-hand side of the road. As I approached, I noted that there were several people wandering around the car looking at the ground. My first thought was that I had a carload of drunks. I pulled off on the road shoulder just to the north of the car, illuminating three men with my headlights and blue emergency lights. As I cautiously approached, I attempted to evaluate what I was stepping into.

Two men who must have been in their seventies came around the car and walked toward me. What struck me was that they were both dressed almost identically. They were wearing clean, bright white button-down dress shirts, rumpled and stained felt fedora hats, equally worn but clean denim bib overalls, and laced-up work boots that appeared to have seen many a day of honest work. The third individual was a young man who looked about eighteen years old. He was very clean cut with no facial hair and was wearing a bit more colorful plaid button-down shirt and jeans that had grass and dirt stains on the knees.

The car was an older model large station wagon, the kind

with wooden sides that could have been referred to as a land yacht. It was sitting at a strange angle in the drainage ditch.

"Boy, am I glad to see you," called out one of the old men.

"Me too!" chimed in the other old fellow.

The young man seemed to mumble something.

I asked who was driving the car, and both old fellows quickly pointed to the young man. "My grandson is driving us," piped up the first old man.

I asked to see the young man's driver's license, and he quickly produced a Virginia permit. "Is this your car?"

"No, it's my great uncle's."

"Do you have his permission to drive it?"

"He sure does," called out the second old man from across the flight deck-sized hood.

I could not find any signs of suspicious or criminal activity nor the telltale signs of drinking alcohol, such as odor or empty bottles. I asked if they had been drinking. and all three were adamant that they were good Baptists and did not drink.

Once that was settled, I asked what was going on. They had been driving down the parkway in the dark and pulled over because the young man's grandfather had to go to the bathroom. When he pulled over, the car slid into the ditch, and they could not get it out. They said they had no money for a wrecker to pull them out, so I thought it might be worth a try to push the car out, since it did not look very stuck. The problem was that the old men, who were brothers, did not know how to drive a car nor could they push, because of health problems. Luckily for my back, a passing vehicle stopped, and two strapping local farm boys that I knew asked if we needed help. Between the three of us pushing, and the old men supervising and directing the young man to go in reverse instead of forward, we were able to free the car with relative ease.

As we were getting the three travelers ready to get back on the road, the grandfather asked me, "How far is it to Lynchburg?"

"Do you mean Lynchburg, Virginia?"

"Yeah, what other Lynchburg is there around here?"

"From here it is about a three-hour drive."

"You got to be kidding. We've been on the road for six hours already."

"Where did you start from?," I asked, knowing that it always took people a lot longer to travel on the Blue Ridge Parkway then they had planned.

"Roanoke," was the answer.

Now I was a bit taken aback. For those of you not intimately familiar with the geography of the region, Roanoke, Virginia, is about fifty-six miles due west from Lynchburg, and it usually takes only an hour or so to drive. We were now standing twenty miles south of the state line and about a hundred miles from Roanoke.

"So how come its three more hours to Lynchburg?," asked the grandfather?

"Right now you're in North Carolina," I answered, with a bit of surprise still in my voice. The three of them stood there with shocked looks on their faces. I had dealt with plenty of lost people before, but this had to be the most off-route travelers I had ever seen. After a little more conversation I found that the trio had journeyed from Lynchburg to Roanoke that morning to visit the grandmother, who was in the hospital for heart surgery. Since the brothers could not drive, they had enlisted the grandson's help. On the return trip they could not find the exact route they took to the hospital and came across the Blue Ridge Parkway. One of the party, they would not own up to which one, said he had heard people say that the Blue Ridge Parkway ran to Lynchburg, which it does not. One hundred miles later they pulled off the road to get stuck in a ditch. I was a bit flabbergasted, to say the least.

I then began the process of determining what would be the safest and quickest route to Lynchburg from this dark, rural mountainside. This was not a set of directions I had been asked for previously. I started to explain about how to return north, look for the signs for Galax, Virginia, and then make several other turns to get on Interstate 77 north. All three looked at me with puzzlement on their faces as if I was speaking a foreign language. They must be tired, I thought, so I got out a map and started pointing out the route. Whenever I got to the part about looking for a sign that said Galax or Interstate 77 I felt I was losing them again. So I got out my note pad and started writing detailed directions to go with the map. I still felt my information was not getting through. I asked the driver if he thought he could find his way. His answer was, "I don't think so."

"How about you fellas?," I asked his uncle and grandfather.

"Nope, we don't get out of Lynchburg much."

I was starting to understand how they got so lost. "Can you follow the directions I have written out here?," I asked.

"Ahhhh, no," answered the driver.

I was becoming a bit frustrated when it dawned on me. "Can you read?"

The young man turned his face down and did not answer. The grandfather finally piped in, "Ain't none of us can read. Grandma is the reader in the family." I finally had my answer to the communications problem. They were so lost because they could not read the road signs. They recognized the Blue Ridge Parkway when they came across it outside Roanoke because of the brown signs with the big national park service arrowhead emblems on them.

I then spent a good half hour or more explaining how to get home. I drew pictures of signs for the Interstate and towns they would pass. It was the best I could do, and they showed a bit more confidence. At last I sent them on their way north in what was at least the right general direction. I never did hear if they made it back to Lynchburg or not, but if they did, I know it took them a long time.

The Snake Man

In 1989, I was on a three-week wildfire detail in Oregon when my wife received a cryptic telephone call from a man who refused to identify himself. He told her that there were large numbers of poisonous snakes being taken from the Blue Ridge Parkway and then sold to several different markets. He did not give much detail or any names of persons that were involved. After I returned home I tried to follow up on this by asking around to other agencies and parks if they had received any reports or information about snake poaching. No one could shed any light on the subject, so I just sat back and kept my ears open.

About two weeks later, an off-duty ranger from Shenandoah National Park was in a pet store when his friend, the shop owner, took him aside to ask a question. He wanted to know if it was legal to sell poisonous snakes. The ranger remembered his supervisor telling him about my inquiry and he instantly became interested. The store owner told the story of a man who had come to the shop and asked if they would be interested in buying any snakes. The owner asked what kind of snakes he was referring to, and the man said, "Any kind you want, but mostly rattlesnakes and copperheads."

When the ranger returned and passed on this conversation to his supervisor, I was contacted. After discussing our options, we called the Virginia State Game Commission's supervisor of covert (undercover) investigations. He was very interested in this case and offered to assist by furnishing us with one of his agents. The pet store owner was given a phone number that went to the agent's home and was told that should the snake salesman return, to give the number to him as a possible snake dealer. Two days later the snake salesman showed up at the pet store and was given the telephone number. Within twenty-four hours he called the agent at his home and started negotiating to sell him rattlesnakes and copperheads. A meeting was set up to look at some of his wares.

The agent went to Staunton, Virginia, where he met Eric Finney and his wife Judy. They all went to the Finney's home, where the agent was shown a room full of aquariums containing a variety of snakes. At that time the agent bought a rattlesnake for thirty dollars. When he asked Finney where he had gotten the snake he said, "From the Blue Ridge Parkway. That's where I get most of my snakes."

The agent asked how he went about the capturing of poisonous snakes and was invited on what turned out to be an interesting evening's ride. Finney's wife, Judy, seven months pregnant at the time, drove the others in the family sedan to the Blue Ridge Parkway after dark. They traveled south at a very slow speed with Eric Finney closely watching the road shoulder. At a certain point he would call for his wife to stop, and before the car came to a standstill he would jump out of the passenger door with a broom handle-like stick with a hook on the end and move into the headlights. When he turned back to the vehicle Finney had a snake draped over the end of the stick. He then moved to the trunk, his wife hit an internal trunk release, and the snake was dumped into a cooler. The trunk was softly closed, and Finney re-entered the vehicle as it started to move. The whole process took less than two minutes.

They moved down the road and pulled into an overlook. Finney marked the location on a map where the snake had been picked up. "We mark all the places we find snakes on the map so we can come back to spots where lots of snakes are and find dens. That way we'll be able to pick up a lot more snakes at one time. Now, ain't that smart?"

After numerous visits with Finney and the purchasing of several snakes, we started to find out a little more about Finney and his past. We found that he had an impressive history of felony convictions for illegal drugs and burglary. His specialty of late was breaking into schools and stealing computer equipment. He was known as "Mr. B&E" (breaking and entering) by the local law enforcement officers. He had even been a deserter from the navy and was convicted for several burglaries in the Chicago area.

Eric's wife, Judy, also had a checkered past that including several felony convictions for bad checks, burglary, and larceny. Evidently she had assisted her husband on several of his crime sprees.

On top of all this, both were involved with satan worship, which was one of their main markets for illegally taken snakes. Other people would buy them for a variety of reasons including as pets, for their skins, for their venom, and for some fundamentalist Christian ceremonies.

The Finneys definitely made for an interesting couple. After gathering all this information and evidence, we decided it was time to take the Finneys in. At that point Eric started to talk about all the marijuana and cocaine that he had access to. The agent was interested in this aspect of the case, since it could lead to other criminals and sources of illegal drugs. After an interagency meeting at the U.S. attorney's office, we determined that the best course of action would be to wait and see what developed.

Soon thereafter Eric told the agent that if he met him on a certain date and time he would take him to a "guy he knew" that would sell them both drugs and guns. It was believed by the local sheriff's department that the "guy" was a person they had been attempting to catch for some time that sold and bought stolen property. Everything looked good for this deal to go down when it was discovered that on the day Eric was to meet the agent he was to report to the Augusta County Jail to serve a weekend sentence for driving on a revoked license. It was the consensus of the group that our case and possible future cases would be best aided if Eric made the firearms transaction. So arrangements were made with the Augusta County Sheriff's Department that when Eric showed up to serve his weekend in jail, he would be told that they did not have room for him and to come back the next weekend.

So the Friday night arrived for the undercover agent to meet Eric at his house and to buy the gun. When he arrived, he found only Eric's wife there, who told him that Eric had to go to jail that weekend and would not be there. The agent knew differently and asked if he could stick around for a while and drink a beer. His plan was to be ready to go when Eric returned after being turned away at the jail. The agent stayed for almost two hours, and Eric still had not shown up. He felt he could not stay much longer without raising suspicions and had to leave. Around the middle of the week the agent contacted Eric and said that he missed him at the house Friday night. Eric then bragged about how he was supposed to go to jail for the weekend, but was turned away due to overcrowding of the cells. Rather than go home, he went on a two-day alcohol and drug-induced binge with some other friends. His wife never suspected a thing.

Our investigative team decided that it was time to take Eric Finney off the streets and out of the park. Both he and his wife were indicted by grand juries for multiple federal and state violations, and arrest warrants were issued for both. We also obtained search warrants for their residence, property, and vehicle. About this time Finney's wife had her baby, so it was decided that rather than place her in custody she would be notified as to when to appear in court.

We assembled our take-down team at the Staunton Police Department at three a.m. Included in the group was a herpetologist from the U.S. Fish and Wildlife Service. There was no telling what species or numbers of snakes we would encounter in the house. During several visits, the agent had also met

Finney's pet boa constrictor. This snake was six to eight feet in length and was allowed to roam free throughout the house. Consequently, the herpetologist was brought in to handle any live snakes we encountered.

We divided into two teams to cover the front and rear of the residence. When we approached at six a.m., all was still, quiet, and dark. As the lead officer, I was designated to do the knock and entry at the front door.

Two other rangers and I crept up the front steps, and I knocked soundly. The door opened a crack, and I could see Eric Finney looking out at me through a four-inch crack. I am not sure why I did this, and all the other officers were surprised, but at that point I just said in my most friendly park ranger voice, "Good morning, Eric. How are you doing?" He looked at me with a surprised look on his face and stepped back. I softly pushed the door open and moved into the room, the two other rangers at my back. Eric continued to step backwards, and as I began to brace for the lunge toward him, I noticed a new-born infant on the floor at my feet. I dodged around the child and grabbed Eric by the arm, informing him, "Eric Finney, you are under arrest."

Finney said he knew it was the police since "No one else would knock like that." He based this on years of experience of having the police knock at his door. He had been surprised and bit startled by my soft and kind demeanor, which threw him off from the attack he was about to launch at me. The backdoor team then entered the house. They had delayed a moment or two because they had not heard any yelling or screaming. Although I would never recommend it, in this case being a nice guy worked out.

During the subsequent search we found six rattlesnakes and two copperheads in aquariums throughout the house. The boa constrictor we found in the freezer. Apparently one night while drinking Eric decided he wanted to see how long it would take the snake to die if he stabbed it in the head. So he brought it into the kitchen and pushed a knife through its head, pinning it to the dining room table. I never did ask him how long it took.

Also found were several containers of snake venom in the refrigerator and small amounts marijuana and other drugs.

While transporting Finney to the local jail he continued to profess his innocence of any crime. He also informed me that they are always putting the wrong people in jail. In fact, he was supposed to report to jail that past weekend but was turned away because it was so overcrowded. I kept a straight face and just responded with, "You don't say."

As we decided earlier, Judy Finney was not placed in custody, having given birth to their first child only a few weeks before. She was given a date and time to report in federal court. With her criminal record she knew she would be going to jail. So the day before her court appearance, she went to a couple she knew that lived in a local trailer park and gave them her baby. Not to babysit, but to keep, since she would be in jail. At her court appearance her appointed attorney begged for her to be kept out of jail due to her needing to care for a newborn infant. Judy was released on a suspended sentence. Three days later, she showed up back in the trailer park for her baby. The couple said she could not have it back because she had given it to them. A fight ensued and the police were called. Judy Finney ended up in jail after all, and her baby was turned over to child protective services.

As for Eric Finney, he was sentenced to almost eight years in federal prison. It did not help his situation that earlier in his criminal career he had deserted from the navy. The federal district court judge that heard his case was a thirty-plus-year naval veteran who retired as a captain.

This case also had significance to the state of Virginia. It was the first time in its history that the Department of Game and Inland Fisheries was involved in convicting a person for wildlife crimes that did not involve a game species. Snakes at that time were not protected under state law nor covered by hunting regulations. Following the outcome of this prosecution the state passed laws to protect snakes and other nongame species from being taken for commercial purposes.

This successful investigation was the result of six law enforcement agencies and jurisdictions working together for a common cause. We so often hear about and see on television where law enforcement agencies are in competition with each other and do not cooperate. This is just one prime example from my career where I found this to be untrue. Without this effort of working together, this couple would have continued to victimize people, our resources, and our school systems.

The Dog That Saved a Life

"The Rescue Squad called and they need you to go to mile post 27 to shoot a dog."

I was a bit stunned by this request at 6:30 a.m. in mid-December 2006, as I tried to cradle the phone with my shoulder and shrug into my body armor and uniform. "What the hell is going on?"

The report was that a man was injured in an auto accident and a dog would not let the rescue squad members get near their patient. The man was not able to respond to his would-be rescuers and they were frustrated.

As I drove to the scene, I kept thinking that there was no way I could destroy someone's dog, especially if it was trying to protect its owner. I started thinking of alternatives such as getting a vet to sedate the dog, but then how long would it take to get someone like that to the accident site?

As I arrived I noted several vehicles in the Big Spy Overlook, including a bear hunter's truck with dog boxes in the bed and hounds heads hanging out of vent holes. An ambulance and a group of people were on the opposite side of the road. As I exited my vehicle I had four people, including two rescue squad members, all trying to talk at once. I heard only bits and pieces such as, "You have to do something," "That dog needs to be killed," and "I did not do anything."

I walked across the road and found a man laying down the bank with his back against a barbed wire fence. His face was covered with blood and he appeared to be attempting to talk, but no sounds other than grunts were coming out. On his chest was a black Labrador retriever growling at the rescue squad members. "You're going to have to shoot him," excitedly blurted one of the squad members. It appeared to me that the dog was just trying to protect his master, in other words, doing his job and doing it well. The last thing he deserved was to die. Besides, I thought the injured man would not want to lose his companion. After looking a bit closer, it looked like the dog also had quite a bit of blood on him, but it was difficult to tell who was doing the bleeding.

I asked the squad members for a back board, a five-foot-long stretcher made of hard polymer plastic. I then used the board to slide the dog off the injured man and then held it between the dog and the patient. I instructed rescue squad members to get to the man, and they quickly checked him out and placed him on a stretcher. He was still unable to talk clearly. A quick examination by the emergency medical technicians showed no indications of obvious physical injuries other than a cut on his head.

I then returned to the dog that was still lying in the ditch and found that he had an injured leg and was bleeding.

It was then time to put my investigator hat on and try to figure out what had happened. When I asked the rescue squad members where the man's wrecked car was, they said they did not know. The only vehicles that were there when they arrived were a Chevy Suburban and the bear hunter's truck in the overlook.

I then went to the hunters that were with the truckload of dogs and asked what they knew. The driver informed me that he had been driving by heading north at around 6 o'clock when he saw something come out of the dark on his right and then felt a thud against his truck. He turned around and came back to see what he had hit. That is when they found the man in the ditch with the dog and called 911 for help. I asked him, but he did not think he had hit the man with his truck. I closely examined the pickup truck and found no damage that would indicate hitting a pedestrian.

I then walked over to check out the unattended Suburban. The vehicle was locked, so I looked in the windows and noticed what appeared to be a dog blanket and leash in the backseat. At the rear of the vehicle leaning against the double doors was a walking stick with blood on it.

I ran a check on the license plate through our dispatcher, and it came back to John and Susan Germanski from Stuarts Draft, Virginia. The dispatcher was able to find a telephone number for the owners, and I called it on my cell phone. The phone was quickly picked up by a woman whose voice revealed her frantic worry. Susan Germanski had been looking for her husband since the previous day when he left the house in their Suburban with their dog, Raider. She explained that her husband suffered from Lou Gehrig's disease and was unable to verbally communicate. I told her that her husband was being transported to the hospital and I would meet her there. I also informed her that Raider was also injured and that I would make arrangements to get him to a veterinarian. An Augusta County animal control officer arrived at the scene and loaded up Raider and transported him to the closest vet.

I then met Susan Germanski at the Augusta Medical Center emergency room. She explained how her husband's disease had been progressing over the past few years and that they had moved to Virginia from New York a year earlier for a slower and more calm life style to reduce his anxiety as his ability to function declined. Raider was his constant companion and went everywhere with him. She was also sure that her husband would never be able to tell us what had happened. Susan gave me the keys to their Suburban and gave me permission to look through the vehicle.

When I returned to Big Spy Overlook, I opened the vehicle and attempted to start the engine. Not only did it not come to life, but I discovered that the vehicle was out of gas. That explained why John Germanski had been there.

As I tried to place the limited puzzle pieces together, I developed the following explanation.

John Germanski had left his home to go for a drive, thinking perhaps that this might be his last time to drive on his own. He ran out of gas at the Big Spy Overlook. I later spoke with a local resident who had seen Germanski at the overlook the evening before, attempting to flag them down. They did not stop because of his "strange appearance" but did not think enough of it to call and report it.

At some point Germanski must have fallen in the dark and hit his head on the stone curb of the overlook parking lot. This was supported by a smear of blood I found on the curb stones. This would account for the blood on the walking stick and the rear door of the Suburban and the cut found by the rescue squad. This would further contribute to Germanski's possible confusion and fear.

The only lights visible from the overlook are across the road and approximately one mile down at the foot of the mountain. It appears that failing to flag anyone down to assist him, Germanski fell in attempting to climb over the barbed wire fence, resulting in his laying up against it. In his weakened condition he was unable to get back up. He then spent the rest of the night in this position.

Raider the Labrador then spent the night lying on top of his master, keeping him warm and protected.

Most likely the first vehicle to drive by the next morning was the bear hunters trying to get an early start to their day. Raider, hearing the approaching truck, went to the road in an attempt to alert them. Once he found that the truck was not going to stop, Raider ran out in front of the truck, resulting in his being struck, breaking his leg. Raider then dragged himself back to his master and barked when the hunter's truck came back around.

If it had not been for Raider, I am convinced that Germanski would have laid there for several more hours, his condition declining before anyone would have noticed him out of view from the road. Raider keeping him warm had also prevented

Germanski from going into hypothermia and shock. Raider was truly a hero, and I am very pleased I had not listened to others and hurt or even killed him. I was also relieved that someone else at the scene had not taken things into their own hands and shot Raider before I got there.

As it turns out, John Germanski was not seriously injured other than the cut on his head. He was kept in the hospital for two days for observation and released with his driver's license suspended for medical reasons. Unfortunately this was another step down in the spiraling decline of his disease and life style.

Raider had a severely broken rear leg and damaged ribs. There was also a fear that he had additional internal injuries. All of this was overwhelming for the Germanskis. A veterinarian in Charlottesville, Virginia, came to the rescue and performed multiple surgeries and provided extended treatment for Raider at no cost to the Germanskis. In my opinion, another hero stepped in to save a hero.

Eventually Raider recovered from his injuries and moved back home with the Germanskis to finish his days, hopefully in the peace and quiet that they came to Virginia to find.

Politics in the National Parks

At times, it becomes hard for the idealist to learn how things are done in the real world. What it takes to make things happen or get done may not always be for the most gallant of reasons. During my career, I saw many instances where policy decisions were made to meet political reality rather than perhaps the best choice based on ethics or mission-driven priorities.

On the Blue Ridge Parkway there is a somewhat controversial program called Hunter Access Permits. Although by regulation and legislation, hunting and the possession of loaded or accessible firearms (in a recent change, Congress has authorized the possession of firearms in national parks starting in February 2010) or wildlife is prohibited within the boundaries of the Blue Ridge Parkway, these permits allow hunters to do both under certain conditions. The way it is designed to work is that a hunter with a permit issued by the park service can carry his or her firearms or bow and arrow unloaded and in a case within their vehicle to a specific designated parking area. They can then take the unloaded weapon to the nearest point on the boundary line directly below the parking area and access legal hunting areas on U.S. Forest Service lands. The hunters can then bring back any game they have taken by the same route and remove it to their homes through the park in their vehicle. The original idea in the 1970s was to allow hunters some access into otherwise remote areas of U.S. Forest Service managed lands to hunt. This sounds simple enough, but it is amazing how complicated it can get.

Several times there has been talk of scaling back the number of access points within the park available to hunters. This is prompted by the increased ease of access using roads that have been built on U.S. Forest Service lands, making many areas not as remote or inaccessible as in the 1970s. There has been no removal of areas for hunter access due to political and special interest pressure placed on the park.

Many of the hunters who use this permit for two months or more a year spend the other ten months thinking up questions and ways to get around the regulations. This makes life hard on the park ranger attempting to filter those people making simple mistakes from those trying to get by with something or just out–and–out breaking the law.

One hunter asked if he would be guilty of possessing a weapon in the park if he was just walking down the road with a shotgun barrel. He claimed that he would not actually have a gun since you cannot shoot anything with just the barrel. I told him that would not work, since his intention was still to hunt. A couple of weeks following the above interview, a ranger caught the same man and one of his buddies walking down the road within the park, each carrying a shotgun barrel. Once it became clear as to what was going on, we found that the trail from the designated parking area to where they wanted to hunt was too steep for their out-of-shape bodies. On the first day of hunting season they had legally carried their weapons into the woods, leaving the stock and receiver part of the guns at their hunting location. After that, they just carried the barrels down the road to where it was easier to walk into their hunting area. The judge did not quite see their logic and convicted them both for violating their permits.

Another hunter tried a similar strategy using a bicycle. The first day of hunting season, he carried his rifle and gear into the woods. At the end of the day he hid all this under a log. The next day he came back with a bicycle and rode it a mile down the parkway from the parking area and then hid it in the woods, walking in to the gear he had hidden. It took a week or so until a hiker reported finding a bike hidden under a tarp just off a trail specifically closed to hunter access. We figured out what was going on but had no luck getting out early enough or staying out late enough to catch our hunter/biker. After several days of this, I had one of the rangers collect the bike as a lost and found item. We filed a report and stored the bike in a secure area. A week after hunting season, a man came in to report losing a bike. The description matched the one we had. I simply told him that we had found it and wanted to keep it safe. I also told him that I hoped he was not using it to gain access for hunting in that trail area. He assured me that he had not, and we never did see him use it for this purpose again.

Then there are bear hunters. The way bears are hunted in this part of the world is a rather high-tech, organized process involving as many as thirty hunters and fifty dogs chasing one bear. These groups are highly organized and make use of radio communications and assigned lookouts so they can remain informed as to the whereabouts of the law. One of the favorite ways of getting on a bear's track is to use what is called a strike dog. A strike dog can be placed on a platform on the front of a pickup truck bumper, on the top of a dog box in the bed of a truck or just walked down the road on a leash. When the dog detects where a bear has crossed the road he begins to bark (what is referred to as strike) at the fresh trail. The rest of the hunters arrive, and they unload dogs to take off after the bear. The dogs are equipped with electronic tracking collars, so the hunter does not even have to enter the woods until the crucial moment when the bear is chased up a tree and the dogs keep it there until the hunters can arrive. While the dogs are running, the hunters are riding around on the surrounding roads with tracking antennas and CB radios monitoring the dogs' movements and directing each other to where the action is going on. Once the dogs stop moving, the hunters know that they have a bear "treed." The hunters then move into the general area, triangulating from several tracking antennas and directing each other by radio. Eventually the hunters gather at the tree, and they decide who gets to kill the bear. The chosen one then steps forward and shoots the bear out of the tree. Where this gets complicated is in attempting to define when a person is hunting, just talking on their CB radio, or just looking for their dogs.

As an example, if you have thirty hunters after a bear, only one gets to shoot the bear, and therefore only one gun is needed. Many bear hunters will not carry a gun with them so that if they are caught in the park illegally they will argue in court that they could not have been hunting since they did not have anything to shoot with. Illegal hunters working out of season or at night may have one person carry an unloaded gun and another person in a separate vehicle carry the ammunition. This way, if they are caught, they can argue that they were not hunting, they were just looking for lost dogs and did not have any way of shooting a bear.

The problem for park rangers is that the Hunter Access Permit gives people a reason to be in the park with weapons, ammunition, and taken wildlife. This complicates the ranger's ability to determine an individual's intent and to catch those killing animals illegally.

Due to hunting being prohibited in most parks, many people that enjoy getting into the outdoors during the fall and early winter and do not hunt look to national park service areas for a safe environment to hike and camp. Many times when visitors arrive at a trail head or parking area on the Blue Ridge Parkway, they are surprised to see hunters with guns and dogs being unloaded where they wanted to take their family. This often causes a conflict between traditional/permitted activities and nontraditional and generally nonpermitted activities such as hunting.

Now enters the U.S. congress. In the early 1990s there was a movement in congress for the park service to generate funding to cover the cost of doing business by charging park user fees. Those parks that already charged an entrance fee would have those fees increased, new areas would charge a fee, and there would be charges for such activities as permits for nontraditional park uses. Up until this point there had been no fees for permits on the Blue Ridge Parkway. It was determined by park management that the first permit to have a fee attached to it would be the Hunter Access Permit. This fee was set at fifteen dollars for the first year.

As soon as word got out to the hunting community that there would be a fee for this permit, well, it would be kind to say "all hell broke loose." There were meetings of hunting groups and clubs, petitions, staged protests on the parkway, threats made against park rangers and management, and ultimately, letters to congressmen.

I have yet to understand fully why, but nothing strikes fear into a park superintendent's heart more than a letter from a congressman. This fear is only amplified when said letter is from a member of the budget committee. At that time there was a congressman from North Carolina that chaired the House Appropriations Committee that simply called the park superintendent and wanted to put a stop to charging hunters for these permits. Hunters were a very vocal and organized constituency in his district. When the superintendent informed him that the fee was levied at the direction of congress to collect funds to pay for administering such programs, the congressman wanted to know how much it cost to run the Hunter Access Program. Thus, overnight numerous park staff scrambled to figure total estimated costs for issuing and enforcing the Hunter Access Permits. This final figure was laid on the congressman's desk within forty-eight hours. The congressman then said that if the park did not charge this fee, he assured the superintendent that the submitted amount would appear in the next budget as a line item to prevent us from having to charge this particular group a fee. This is an example of what is referred to as pork barrel legislation that only serves a small area or portion of our nation. In some media outlets this would more specifically be referred to as "park barrel" legislation. In addition the congressman became interested in funding a major construction project on the parkway, a new headquarters building in Asheville, North Carolina, located in his voting district. This interest was dependent on whether the park could make the hunters happy. The congressman was quoted as saying, "Find someone else to charge a fee."

Prior to the beginning of the next hunting season, we were informed that there would not be a fee charged for Hunter Access Permits. In addition, the park had to completely redesign the permit process to make it easier for hunters to obtain the permit. This new system had to be approved by the congressman's office before implementation. In addition, park rangers received a memo from the chief rangers office, directing them to be understanding and courteous to hunters that season due to the repercussions of the year before. After that year, any changes even of wording in the Hunter Access Permit System would have to be approved by this congressman before being implemented. This often resulted in delays in getting the permits printed for the year and lethargy from the park staff to make any changes or conduct reviews of the system.

The following year, 4.2 million dollars was appropriated for the beginning construction of the new park headquarters. The Blue Ridge Parkway never received any additional funding to administer the Hunter Access Permit program. Fees did start to be charged to people requesting a permit to be married in the park. Commercial operations such as filming and vehicle transport saw new and increased permit fees. Hunter Access Permits remained free, and there is no more talk of scaling back on hunter use of the Blue Ridge Parkway.

This is just one rather minor example of how special interest groups that have political connections can affect national park service policy and regulations. There are many larger scale and longer range damaging examples throughout the system. The challenge for today's managers is to find a balance between these politically motivated pressures and the preservation of our cultural and natural resources for future generations. It takes a dedicated and brave person to make such a stand, and luckily these people do still exist. A significant number have had careers destroyed or ended for making a stand based on principles and ethics. I am proud to have worked with several such individuals during my career.

Creative Justice

"What was that?"

RING.... RING! The fog began to clear from my head and I realized that the telephone was ringing. I rolled over and looked through my sleep-crusted eyes at the alarm clock. The green illuminated digits read 2:15 a.m. This time of the morning, it could only be an emergency in the park.

"Hello, this is Bruce Bytnar."

"This is the Parkway Emergency Dispatch. We have a call from the Waynesboro Police Department. Something about an assault or something. Should I patch you through?"

"Yeah, go ahead." I tried to shake the cobwebs of sleep from my head as the phone lines clicked in my ear. I seemed to recall that I had worked twelve hours the day before and had been in bed less than three hours.

"Hello...somebody there?"

"Yea, this is Bruce Bytnar. What do you have for me this bright morning?" At least my sense of humor was starting to wake up.

"This is Officer Slocum with the Waynesboro PD. We have two people down here who claim to have been assaulted and robbed in the park."

"Where did this supposedly happen?," I asked, knowing that often people got the location of incidents confused. I had been awakened numerous times for happenings that did not even occur on park service property.

"They said the second overlook. I think the woman may have been sexually assaulted."

"Are they there at your office now?"

"Yeah, they are in the back."

"Hold them there until I can get in."

"Okay. Are you coming here?"

"Yeah, I'll be there as soon as I can."

The line went dead, and my mind started to click. I put my finger in the cradle, lifted, and got a dial tone and started pressing numbers. After three rings a rough voice answered, "Yeah, what is it?"

"Lew, Bruce."

"What happened now?"

"We had report of an assault and robbery at Rockfish Valley Overlook. Get up there, check it out, and secure the scene. I'm going to Waynesboro PD to interview the victims."

"Okay, talk to you later." Click.

Fifty-two minutes later, I was sitting behind a gray metal institutional desk in a small room badly in need of painting or at least a good cleaning. Across from me sat a man and a woman nervously squirming in their uncomfortable industrial plastic chairs. The woman had obviously been crying and the man was alternating between flicking his butane lighter and touching the woman, making a weak attempt to abate her anguish. Both were smoking like chimneys. I hate being around cigarette smoke, and my mood darkened.

"I know this may be hard to talk about right now, but the more you can tell me the better the chances we have to catch this guy. So if you can, start from the beginning, and tell me what happened on the parkway?"

They gave a quick glance to each other and then the woman started, "Well, we met tonight at Lynn's They had a band there tonight, and we were dancing and drinking."

"Not that we got drunk or anything," the lighter flicker interrupted.

"You were sloshed. That's why I had to drive." The man cowered back into his chair. "Anyway, when the place closed we decided to go up to the parkway and have a few more beers and...you know." I nodded my head in what I hoped appeared a worldly way.

"Okay so what happened once you got to the parkway?"

"Well, we stopped at the second overlook..."

"You mean the Rockfish Valley Overlook?"

"Yeah, I think that's the one. You'll know because my car is still up there. The guy stole my keys."

"Okay, we'll get to that. So what happened in the overlook?"

"We got out of the car and were lying on the grass in front of the car..."

"Yea, we were really getting into it, and well, screwing," he added.

She gave him another sharp look and then turned back to me. "Okay, we were buck naked. Does that make you happy?" She glowered at her companion, and he once again sunk deeper into the recesses of the hard plastic chair. I just gave a nod of my head in her direction as a clue for her to continue. "Anyway, we were there and I did not hear any vehicles or see any lights when all of a sudden I felt something against my head and a man's voice say, 'get up bitch.' I turned and saw a big black man standing over me with a gun pointed in my face."

"What did the gun look like?"

"It was silver and kinda small because I could see it was small in his hand."

I turned to the man. "Did you see the gun?"

"No, I never got a good look at it." He was being sheepish now and not as willing to fill in gaps with more information.

"That's because you spent most of your time hiding in the bushes."

I was starting to remember how in basic law enforcement school they always taught you to separate people before you interview them. I was starting to understand another reason why that was a good idea. "Okay, so after you saw the gun, what did you do?"

"I screamed and we both ran down the hill into the briers. The man then yelled for me to come back up. I tried to hide as best I could. He then called out that he could see Joey and if I did not come back up to him that he would shoot him." The story was really starting to flow fast now as her excitement to get it all out rose. "Then the next thing I know Joey is yelling for me to get up the hill. I said no way and then saw two bright flashes and heard two gun shots. I heard Joey scream and I ran up the hill." Tears were starting to come to her eyes now. Joey was not looking so good either.

"When I got back up to the man he pointed the gun in my face made me get down on my knees, and I tried to cover myself. He told me not to move and picked up our clothes and started going through the pockets. He took some things and put them in his pockets. He kept saying that if I moved he was going to kill me and that he was already in enough trouble tonight that it would not matter if he shot me. He then went around and reached into the car. I heard my keys, and he took out my purse. He came back around the front and took our clothes and threw them over the bank. He then came back over to me and put the gun to my head." At this point she started to choke a little. Joey leaned forward and gave a more sincere show of support, and she fell against him.

"Can you continue or would you like to take a break?"

"No, no. It's okay. He started to pull down his zipper in front of my face and said he wanted me to put him in my mouth. I told him I did not do that type of thing and he asked me if I wanted to die. I tried to keep talking to him, and he kept going on about his being in so much trouble already that it did not matter what he did. All of a sudden he looked up and said, 'lights.' He then turned away from me and started to walk quickly like away. I stood up and he turned back toward me, pointing the gun right at my face. I was so scared I fell to the ground. As I fell I heard the gun go off two or three times, I don't know for sure, and I thought I was dead." She stopped to catch her breath.

"Did you get a good look at him? Could you identify him if you saw him again?"

"Well, unfortunately my glasses were in the car and I'm blind without them."

I turned to Joey. "How about you?"

"I was in the briars the whole time. All I saw was his silhouette. He looked big though, but not fat. And he was definitely black."

The word "great" ran through my head. This was not going to be easy although I already had a suspect in mind. We had charged a black male the year before for peeping in cars of young lovers parked in the overlooks in that area. In one case a ranger caught him masturbating against the exterior of a couple's car.

The woman caught her breath, choked back her tears, and told me the rest of their story. Once the suspect left them, they were naked, their clothes spread down the side of the mountain, and no keys to their car. Several of their friends were "partying" in the next overlook to the north of them along the parkway. So they walked naked for over a mile along the road to find their friends. They all then returned to the scene of the crime only to find no sign of the criminal. They then got a ride to the woman's home, where they picked up some clothes and went to the police department.

For some reason this entire tale reminded me of one person, the same black male we had arrested before in this same area, Darnell Smote. Smote lived in a nearby small city and was a main suspect in a series of rapes in that jurisdiction. The problem local police kept running into was that the victims were afraid to identify or testify against their attacker. Later that morning I contacted the Staunton, Virginia, Police Department and met with two of their detectives. They were very familiar with Smote and agreed with my suspicion that this sketchy description could be him. Unfortunately, we did not have enough evidence to justify a search warrant or arrest.

Later that day the male victim from the night before called me at my office. He told me that he had a cloth bag with some

bullets in it that he and his friends had picked up the night before after he was attacked, if I wanted it. I said of course and left
immediately to meet him at the entrance to the park at Rockfish
Gap. As I pulled up I noted that there were six men surrounding a Nelson County deputy. As I approached I experienced a
sinking sensation in my stomach as I saw that the deputy was
holding a purple Crown Royal bag in his one hand with several bullets in his palm. He was picking up each bullet in his
ungloved hands and looking them over. My hopes of valuable
evidence dissipated further. I asked why the evidence had not
been turned over the night before and was told that they had
forgotten about it. The deputy was adamant that he keep the
bag and bullets. I just shook my head in disgust and told him
that I would arrange to have the fingerprints of our suspect forwarded to him to send to the lab. I knew that after the bullets
had been handled by so many people, there was little chance of
getting a fingerprint match with anyone.

I thought I was going to get home for some needed sleep
when the dispatcher called me over the radio. He said that a
woman had called from Waynesboro, Virginia, and that she
might have some information related to what had happened
the night before in the park. She said that she would meet me
at the Waynesboro Police Department.

Apparently the victims I had interviewed were not the only
ones to meet with problems the night before. This young lady
had gone to the same overlook earlier in the evening with a
man she had met at the restaurant she worked at. They were
parked, looking at the view and necking, when she felt his
hand crawling up her thigh. She pushed the hand away and
said, "No," and her date sat back. After a few minutes rest they
started necking again and eventually she felt the hand crawling back up her leg. This time she yelled, "No," and grabbed
the hand. When she looked down she was surprised to find
that it was not the hand of her date but the arm of black man
outside the vehicle reaching in through the open window. Now
her protest increased in intensity, she screamed, and she threw
the arm away, trying to crawl into the backseat.

Her date jumped out of the car, running around and attempting to grab the groper. The black male ran toward the only other car in the overlook, and the date continued after him. Without warning the black male stopped, turned, and pointed a handgun at the date, saying he would kill him. The date stopped in his tracks, and the suspect jumped in his car and drove off.

The female victim could not describe the suspect other than that he was a black male that looked athletic, had no facial hair, and was wearing what looked like a warm-up suit. This was very little to go on, and she did not think she would recognize her attacker if she saw him. As for the date, all she knew was that his first name was Steve and that he said he worked for the DuPont Company. Steve was from out of town and was visiting on business. I checked with the local DuPont factory, and they did not have any employees or contractors from out of town that week. So that was a dead end.

The woman was able to give a good description of the car the suspect was driving. Apparently, it was an old, antique-looking car, possibly a Rambler, and turquoise in color. This was the first real break in the investigation.

I then went back to the Staunton Police Department to share this new information with them. They were very interested since they had information that Darnell Smote had been seen driving an antique turquoise Rambler that belonged to a professor at a local college. I then had Lew, the ranger that had helped me the night before, go to the restaurant that Smote was working at, where he found the turquoise Rambler. From a distance, Lew took photos of the car, and we had them developed at a one-hour photo shop. With these photos I prepared a line-up of twelve sedans, all greenish to turquoise in color. My second victim without hesitation picked out the Rambler we had photographed as the car her assailant had fled in.

Even with this information the assistant U.S. attorney still did not feel we had enough information to arrest our suspect, Darnell Smote. We were able to obtain a search warrant for his apartment and the Rambler. Inside the car we found a pistol holster but no gun. No other property belonging to the victims or the weapon were found in the apartment. The lab report on the bullets in the bag came back with no evidence to tie them to anyone. We again met with the prosecutors, and they still did not feel that we had enough evidence to arrest Smote. Without a positive identification of the suspect or definitive physical evidence, they did not feel we had a case. I met again with the victims, but none of them were able to identify Smote out of a group of six photos of black males that were similar to the vague descriptions we had.

While meeting with the Staunton detectives again to discuss our next course of action, an offhand comment was made that Smote was still on probation for a drug charge. I found this to be of interest and was able to get the name of Smote's probation officer, who I immediately contacted.

I described our interest in Smote, and the probation officer became animated with excitement. He had been suspicious of Smote since he had returned from prison, obtaining probation after a conviction for trafficking in cocaine. Smote was suspected of continuing his criminal activities and had been a suspect in at least one rape since coming back to town. It was decided to call Smote in immediately and subject him to a drug test. If he came back positive, his probation could be administratively revoked. That same day Smote reported as requested to the probation office and was instructed to give a urine sample for drug testing. At first, he tried to make excuses of why he could not, but none of them were valid. He submitted the sample under the watchful eye of the probation officer, and it tested as positive for cocaine and marijuana. Apparently Smote had been cheating on his previous drug screenings by smuggling in a sample of someone else's urine to submit for the test. Smote's probation was immediately revoked, and he was taken into custody on the spot.

Two days later I attended a state court hearing where the revocation of Smote's probation was formalized, and he was sent back to prison to serve the remaining eight years of his drug-trafficking term. Although we could never gather enough evidence to charge Smote for his crimes on the Blue Ridge Parkway, we were able to get him into prison and out of the area for eight years. In the balance of justice, Smote ended spending more time in jail for his probation violation than he would if convicted for the assaults that I investigated.

When he returned to the same area eight years later, he immediately became a suspect in a series of rapes on the campus of the University of Virginia. I met with the university police investigators several times to discuss Darnell Smote. Once again, none of the victims could identify their assailant or were afraid to testify against him. As far as I know, Darnell Smote is still out in society somewhere, and I am afraid there will be more victims to his crimes.

The Summer That Burned

The year 1988 was one of the worst on record up to that time for forest fires in our national parks. Every night on the news there were lead stories on the millions of acres of fires burning in the area of Yellowstone National Park. What most people do not realize is that an event of this magnitude in national parks as distant as Yellowstone has a great impact on park service areas as far away as the East Coast. During this time I was stationed on the Blue Ridge Parkway in Virginia, and we started sending firefighters to Yellowstone in early August. None of these personnel were being released once they got to Yellowstone, and we kept getting calls for more and more help. When conditions continued to deteriorate, the director of the national park service declared the Yellowstone fires a nationwide agency disaster, and all qualified personnel were to be released for fire duty out west.

I had served on numerous western fire details during my career, and up to this point, I had been sending less experienced and younger personnel to the fires to give them the opportunity to develop their own skills and knowledge. I was staying behind to keep things together on the home front. I received a call at my office one afternoon informing me that I would be leaving for fire duty the next day. When I attempted to protest due to the lack of personnel left in my district, I was overruled and ordered to go as a crew boss in charge of twenty firefighters.

The national park service, like all federal and many state level land management agencies, is part of the Interagency Wildfire Coordinating Group that is headquartered in Boise, Idaho. The way this nationwide system works is that when there is a forest fire anywhere in the United States and assistance is needed beyond what is available in the immediate area, firefighting resources can be called in from all over the country. All agencies that participate in this system have employees who are put through specific training programs to qualify for different jobs on a fire. These can range from firefighters to supply clerks to emergency medical services personnel. What this means to a park ranger is that they are subject to call for fires from Alaska to the Virgin Islands. Over the years I was sent to fires in Florida, Idaho, Oregon, Utah, Arizona, and California. When firefighters and support personnel are brought in on a fire, the organization closely resembles a military operation. No matter what your job or position status back home, you work in the job that you are assigned.

Being a crew boss on a wildfire detail can be interesting and challenging, to say the least. You normally get to an airport staging area, and that is where you meet the nineteen other people who you will be spending twenty-four hours a day with for possibly the next twenty-one days or more. During this time, you will be responsible for their well-being, morale, work production, safety, and, what is often most difficult, their location at all times. Every group I have ever gone on fires with has at least one "wanderer" who just wants to see what is around the next corner or the next horizon. Most people who go out on fires for the first time are not accustomed to the military type of regimen necessary to ensure their safety. Often they may even try to rebel against this requirement and, thus, the "wandering syndrome" will start to appear in their behavior.

The crew boss keeps all the documentation for the crew members, including the all-important payroll forms. It is a government job, and there is a lot of paperwork. Without these papers, no one gets paid. To give some idea of how important payroll accounting can be, I have never been on a fire where someone has not brought a calculator so they can become an instant accountant and check the records to make sure they get all that is due them.

Whenever I first gather a new crew together, one of the early items on my agenda is, "Who is the most important person on this crew?" The appropriate answer of course is I am, the crew boss, because I am the keeper of payroll and time. If I burn up, so do their payroll records. This often helps to break the ice with a good laugh, but I have to admit that I like the fact that once we are out on the line fighting fire, there are always one or two people who are not quite sure if I was pulling their leg or not, and they always seem to be looking out for my well-being.

On this particular adventure, I was placed in charge of a crew made up of employees from all over the southeast region. We gathered in Roanoke, Virginia, and started the inevitable game of hurry up and wait. When you think about it, it is not easy to suddenly move thousands of firefighters all over the country when you do not have your own air fleet. Planes have to be chartered or commercial tickets purchased, and this co-ordination takes time. So as a result, even though everyone arrived in Roanoke by eight o'clock in the morning, we ended up sitting in a World War II era Quonset hut all day. We finally were put in a motel for the night and returned to the airport, where we sat for another day.

During this time we were told that we would be going to Yellowstone National Park to help with the fires there. We spoke with several people who had already been out on these fires that summer and checked the weather forecasts for the area. All this indicated that things were pretty hot in that area, not only from the fires but from high temperatures. As a result, we did not expect any harsh conditions when we would arrive at our final destination.

Finally, word came that a plane was coming to pick up our

one hundred plus fire personnel and take us to Idaho Falls, Idaho. The problem was that there was not enough room on the plane for all the crews, and as a result our crew was to fly out on a regular commercial flight. We were to arrive in Idaho three hours before the rest of our group and wait for them at the airport. Someone was to meet us and take care of us until the rest of the crews showed up.

We finally arrived in Idaho Falls at ten o'clock at night, and no one was there to greet us. The crew was pretty exhausted from all the traveling and excitement of going on a fire detail, so they lined up their gear along the wall of the terminal and fell asleep.

About an hour later a person from the forest service showed up and told me that we could not stay in the terminal and to follow him to a staging area. We gathered up our gear and stepped out into the night. The first thing that struck us was that it was downright cold out. The temperature was in the mid-thirties, and having come from a heat wave in Virginia in the upper nineties, we were definitely chilled to the bone. I commented on the temperature to the person leading us to the staging area, and his only comment was, "Oh yeah, the weather has changed." What I did not realize at the time is what this would mean to our crew over the next few weeks.

When we arrived at the staging area we found that it consisted of a grassed lawn with two port-a-johns right next to the runway. I told our guide that it was a bit cold to be sitting out on the grass for several hours, and his response was for us to wrap up in our sleeping bags and wait for the rest of the crews to arrive. He then got into his truck and drove off before I could even ask him about food. I turned around and looked into nineteen tired, miserable faces and felt that this situation was ridiculous. In looking around, I noticed the lights on in a private aircraft building about one hundred yards down the runway. Following some brief negotiations, the mechanics on duty let us lay out on the floor of the pilots' lounge to sleep. This was great, but the problem was that when the guide came back to check on us, we were gone. I think he thought we had flown back to Virginia (I have to admit we were tempted), and it took him a while to track us down.

The rest of the crews arrived by six o'clock in the morning, and we were eventually loaded onto busses to be taken to the fire base camp. As we were loading up, I was informed that we were not going to Yellowstone but to a new fire that had just broken out on the Challis National Forest in Idaho. No one on the bus had any idea where this was, so we rode off in sleepy innocence.

After leaving paved roads, we traveled another two hours through the dark in clouds of dust, eventually pulling into what looked like an old ranch from a John Wayne movie. It was past midnight, and as I stepped off the bus to check in with the facilities manager, it could not escape my notice that the temperature was significantly lower than in Idaho Falls, and the harsh, blowing wind contained a substantial amount of snow. We had to wake up several people just to let them know that we had arrived. The first thing I noticed on meeting these fire veterans was that they were wearing nice, warm parkas and hats. I was standing there in my sweatshirt and poplin jacket, already beginning to shiver. Someone finally lit a gas lantern, and everyone unconsciously moved a little closer, attempting to grab what little heat they could.

What I learned at this first meeting forebode of what the future held for us. This was a very low priority fire of only seventy-five thousand acres, and it was proving difficult to obtain supplies and equipment with the demands of the huge fires burning in and around Yellowstone. It was decided that since it was so cold, the arriving fire crews would sleep on the busses until the sun came up and the temperatures rose a little. When the sun finally appeared, the wind picked up, although the snow dissipated, and it warmed up to about 40 degrees. We filed off the bus, still travel worn and seat sore, and were told that there were no tents available. Supply had rolls of plastic, and we were to build our own shelters and try to get some sleep.

I wish I had a video of this group of exhausted and shivering easterners trying to erect a plastic sheet lean-to in a twenty mile an hour wind that decided to spit snow at us again. Somehow we were able to build at least one side of a shelter, and everyone got out their sleeping bags and tried to get some rest. As soon as everyone got somewhat settled, the wind shifted direction and blew right down our line of weary bodies. Two of us then hiked back over to the supply unit to attempt to get some more plastic. There we were met by the supply manager, who refused to give us any more plastic due to the fact that we had received proper allotment for twenty people. About this time, several other newly arrived crew bosses approached to make the same request. They also were denied and cussed out for attempting to waste government money. One of the other crew bosses was a Native American with a crew from his tribe. When he tried to protest this treatment the supply manager said, "Now look here chief." The reaction of the crew boss made me think that I was going to see my first real-life scalping. I very diplomatically stepped out from between these two and even thought of offering the crew boss my pocket knife. Fortunately, or unfortunately, several of his crew members physically held him back. At this point the supply manager's boss showed up and ordered him to give us all the plastic we needed. The manager finally grudgingly issued the sheets of plastic, but not before he informed us that every bit of it would be accounted for when we left to go home. After that incident I was always nervous about going to the supply area. I had visions of standing there arguing with this guy when suddenly flaming arrows started to rain in.

We finally got our shelter built, but things still seemed to go downhill from there. As the days passed, the weather worsened, getting colder and windier. Our base camp was located at around ten thousand feet elevation, and where we worked was over twelve thousand feet. The warmest day we had during our stay here was about forty-two degrees. Several nights the temperatures went down into the single digits, and we still did not get any tents or other forms of shelter. We all began feeling a bit like lost orphans.

They did have a food service contractor to provide meals while we were in camp. It was so cold and the wind blew so hard that when you got to the table to eat, your food was ice cold. The food service people were having a hard time of it themselves. This was the first fire they had been on, and they had not counted on a four-hour, one-way drive to the closest grocery store. As a result, they kept running short on everything, and meals were a bit of an adventure in themselves. One of the favorites was scrambled eggs with cut-up hotdogs left over from the night before. Luckily for me, after two days they put out a large can of Mexican hot sauce, and I put this on everything I ate. It added a little flavor, and even if it did not warm me up, at least it made me sweat a little. Breakfast and supper were at the base camp. Lunch we carried in with us on the line each day.

Every morning I had to be up and dressed by 3:30 a.m. and at a work briefing meeting at 4:00 a.m. The crew would get up at 4:15 and be in line for breakfast by 4:30. This breakfast line was about four hundred people long by 4:45. Usually, I would finish up the briefing and talking to our supervisor for the day by 5:00 a.m. At the briefing I would get details about the day's work assignments, the weather conditions, hazards, and everything else we would need to know to survive the day. After the briefing, I would have to go and line up transportation for my crew, get some crew members to go with me to check out tools, assign someone to pick up bag lunches, account for everyone, and be sure everything was ready to go on a school bus by 5:15. Somewhere in there, if I had time, I would grab some food and throw it into my pack to eat on the bus for breakfast.

We would travel on a school bus for half an hour and then unload and reload onto military two-and-a-half-ton trucks. We would ride in the back of these open trucks at a snail's pace for about forty-five minutes. Then we would unload and pack up all our gear to be hand-carried to the work site. As per the way our luck was running, on this assignment we worked in the most remote part of the fire. Once we left the trucks, we had to hike straight up a mountain for a 1,500-foot rise in elevation through a burned area of forest. By the time we reach the fire-line where we were assigned, every crew member was covered with black soot, and it was after ten o'clock in the morning.

We would then work through the day, performing back-breaking work constructing a fireline by hand, and start back down the mountain by about 6:00 p.m. By the time we got to the base camp, it was usually 8:30, and the temperatures had plummeted again. Once back in camp, I had to be sure that all the equipment for the day was turned in and then attend a de-briefing. By the time I could think about eating, it was usually about 9:00 p.m. After that I would usually fall into my sleeping bags and try to fall asleep.

By the second week the supply unit had loosened up a bit, and we were all sleeping in at least three layers of sleeping bags. These bags were made out of paper and were disposable. They hardly compared to a real sleeping bag, but it was all we had. Everyone slept in every piece of clothing they had and were still cold. I distinctly remember one night laying there in all my clothes and sleeping bags and wondering to myself if I would ever see my wife and son or eat pizza again. After that night no one in the crew was allowed to use the word pizza again (although I know they whispered it behind my back).

Sanitation was deplorable in that we did not have a place to wash our hands for the first five days. We went without show-ers for twelve days. Luckily, there were plenty of port-a-johns available. There was a bank of about twenty of them in a single line. It is funny how when on fires under these types of con-ditions, people will have a tendency to latch onto something they can call their own, even if it is a port-a-john. After a while, most individuals will pick out a john they feel most comfort-able with, and that will be the only one they use. I have seen others and even caught myself standing exhausted, waiting for someone to finish with "my port-a-john" while ten or more oth-ers sat empty next to it.

One morning a reporter from the *Washington Post* showed up at our base camp. He wanted to interview firefighters from the Virginia area. I thought there was going to be a stampede of people fighting to be interviewed so they could sit for a few minutes in his heated rental car. I know one person on my crew from Florida tried to say he was from Washington, D.C., just to get in the car for a few moments of relief from the cold. Unfortunately for him, he was crushed as he reached for the door handle when another crew member told on him.

Needless to say, under conditions like these, it did not take long for people to get sick. In fire camps, once one person gets sick it does not take long for it to spread. In this instance, everyone started coming down with sinus infections and related respiratory problems. It was soon evident that the fire emergency medical personnel were not going to be able to handle these types of problems. Every morning they would load up at least one whole bus of sick people and take them into the hospital. A little better than half would come back each evening with a pocketful of pills and elixirs. Illness was so rampant that on one day, out of twenty people on my crew, only eleven were fit to work. I heard through the rumor mill that the head of the emergency medical unit wanted to bring in a doctor or public health official to inspect the camp. The overhead team that was running the operation refused, for fear that such a move would shut firefighting efforts down. Consequently, the conditions continued to deteriorate.

Once we had a fireline completely around the fire and it looked like it was going to snow enough to put it out for the winter, we thought we would be going home. I went in for our briefing expecting to be told they would be sending us to Idaho Falls, only to discover that they intended to send us back out to the 12,000-foot elevation area to rebuild a trail that had been damaged by a bulldozer. I looked up toward the mountain that we were supposed to work on and saw that it was shrouded from view by falling snow. I took my supervisor for the day aside and asked him what good it would do to send a group of sick people up there to work on a trail covered by snow that we probably would not be able to find anyway. He just looked up at me and said, "What is your crew, a bunch of wuzzies or something?" Unbelievably, I kept my cool, which was even harder to believe later when I found out that I had a temperature of 104 at the time.

Being the dedicated or foolish person that I am, I loaded up what was left of the effectives in my crew into the school bus, and we started up the mountain roads. As we were approaching our drop point, a speeding pickup truck swung around us and flagged the bus down. The supervisor jumped out of his truck and onto the bus. He stood in front of this group of haggard sick and said, "Well, the division supervisor says there's too much snow to risk you eastern wimps on working today, so I guess it won't bother you if we send you back to camp." With this, he turned and jumped off the bus. Three of my crew's reaction was to go after him, but he was in his truck and gone before they could reach the front of the bus.

When we got back, I stormed off the bus and tracked down the incident commander (the person in overall charge of the fire) and in quite undiplomatic and colorful verbiage told him what I thought about this fire and some of his staff. With this, he informed me that the fire was being declared controlled due to the weather and that all the crews were going to be moved back to Idaho Falls that evening or the next morning. We did not leave until the next day, when the snow came down even harder. By this time there was not a healthy person among us. Everyone was coughing and hacking as they entered the bus to freedom. I have never felt more relieved than when we left that place.

To culminate our trip, we were not given the time to take showers or clean up in town, and no one had washed any clothes in over two weeks. They then crammed about two hundred firefighters on one plane and flew us all the way back to Roanoke, Virginia.

I should add that not all western fire details are this strenuous. I have been on several that although they involved long hours and hard work, the living conditions were much better and healthier. After several other crews came back east from fires, I spoke with some friends about their experiences. One crew had been on a fire in Montana the same time we were on this one in Idaho. Their fire camp consisted of a Dude Ranch using the guest rooms for a barracks. A congressman or someone else from a high Washington level was coming to visit the area, and the managers did not want him to see firefighters living in such luxury. So they set up a tent city, and everyone moved their gear into it for one day. After the visit they all moved back into the Dude Ranch. I found this perplexing since during this same time they could not even get one tent for the fire we were on.

To this day everytime I run into someone that was on this fire with me, the stories start to fly, and I have to admit a few of them still make me shiver a bit.

Lost in the Woods

When people visit national parks they are most often entering an environment very different from home, where they are used to navigating their daily lives. They may be very efficient at finding their way around the town or city they live in, but put them in the woods on the side of a mountain and all their natural instincts and sense of direction shut down. Often the results are people getting separated and lost. These incidents of "lostness" can last for a few hours to overnight and often result in tension and in some cases panic, which contributes to the deterioration in their ability to make decisions. Add to this the fact that in the mountains, nighttime temperatures drop dramatically, even in summer, and can result in hypothermia. Among the early manifestations of hypothermia is confusion and disorientation. Occasionally, searches can go for longer periods, depending on the complexity of factors and how much the lost person keeps moving. A stationary person is much easier to find, but most people have an instinct to keep moving, hoping to find their own way out.

The national park service spends millions of dollars a year in search operations spanning from children getting separated from their parents to complex technical rescues in such places as Mount Rainier and the Grand Canyon. Scout groups have notoriously provided rangers with opportunities to practice their search skills. Many of these searches result from poor or total lack of leadership and supervision of scouts. Some larger parks have put group size limits on backcountry camping permits in order to eliminate scout groups. In one case a scout was forced by his parents to go camping with this troop. He was unhappy at being separated from his Gameboy and television, so he walked off. The result was a three-day search involving hundreds of searchers and multiple agencies, all seen on national television. The monetary costs were astronomical, and it was suspected that the scout was hiding from searchers the entire time.

The National Park Service has to absorb all the expenses of search and rescue operations. It has even been proposed that when the search and rescue is the result of the violation of regulations, that the subject can be charged for expenses. This has been shot down by congress each time it is brought up. These policies place a great burden on the national park service's budget and time. Many people develop the attitude that if I get lost, a park ranger will instantly come find me. This can produce a false sense of security that results in a lack of personal responsibility. People with these attitudes will often take chances they would not normally think of trying. Often national park service, cooperating agency, and volunteer personnel place their lives on the line to perform these searches and rescues. Many have been injured and in some instances lost their lives trying to save others.

One area I worked where we experienced many short-term and overnight searches was Humpback Rocks on the Blue Ridge Parkway. The complexity of the numerous trails in this area combined with the many unofficial and illegal shortcut trails contribute to people getting lost. There are several common causes that most often result in someone getting lost.

In every group, there seems to be the macho person that has to prove they are bigger, badder, and faster than anyone else. They tend to speed ahead and leave everyone else behind. One part of the group will then get off on a different trail, they get separated, and eventually someone makes it back to civilization and reports the others as lost.

Another example is the family or group with children that let some of the kids run ahead. This usually ends up with different parts of the group taking different trails. When children are lost, everyone has a tendency to overreact, at times justifiably, and run around trying to find them. This usually results in more people getting lost.

The third situation, which often contributes to the two above, is when someone gets in a hurry or is confused and leaves the established trail and tries to go cross-country. Once you leave a trail in the mountains, it is not as easy as it may seem to find your way back. You may not be on the side of the mountain you think you are on or in a different drainage.

Another factor that complicates searches is the good intentions of others. It is important to have control and containment of an area where the search is to be conducted. People running around on hiking trails will destroy valuable evidence such as footprints, tracks, litter, and such left by the lost party. They also taint the scent left by the lost person, which can be critical if the decision is made to use search dogs. I have always instructed new park rangers that their first priority is to gain control of the situation and of all the resources that respond, including local agencies and volunteers. Organization and a plan most often result in quick and safe resolutions to searches.

Other circumstances that complicate a search are weather conditions including predicted upcoming changes, physical condition of the lost subject, health concerns including medications and medical conditions, experience level of the missing person, how the person is equipped and clothed, and how many trained personnel are available to assist.

All searches for lost persons are treated as emergencies and serious business. There are many, however, that end up having human and sometimes humorous twists.

In one instance, we were called to Humpback Rocks by a report of a young lady and her younger brother, who were separated from their group and had been missing for six hours. It was after dark, and the temperature was dropping. Even in the summer, hypothermia is a concern when people are not properly dressed for the elements and the change in temperature. We called out six park service employees and had members of three fire departments and rescue squads show up. We were organizing and started a briefing at the visitor center when I noted two people in the back of the gathering group listening and paying strict attention. After I started the briefing, it finally dawned on me why they looked somehow familiar. It turns out that it was the young lady and her brother we were getting ready to search for. They had found their way out of the woods on their own and came over to see what all the hubbub was about. Figuring out that we were getting ready to go out searching for someone that was lost, they wanted to help, not realizing that we would be looking for them. These two had gone ahead of the rest of their group on the way back to the cars, had gotten off on a nondesignated or social trail, and got turned around. They then tried to get out by going cross-country. A fifteen-minute hike had turned into an eight-hour ordeal.

Another time there were two couples that went for a hike at Humpback Rocks and got off on a wrong trail, tried to go cross-country back to their cars, and ended up going in almost the opposite direction in the dark. We finally found them just after daylight. They had become cold during the night and thought they might freeze to death, even though it was August. In their debriefing, they stated that they burned all their paper money attempting to get a fire going. I asked them if they were carrying any hundred dollar bills. Luckily for them, the highest denomination they burned was a twenty.

I was driving down the Blue Ridge Parkway toward the Peaks of Otter one time when a lady in the Sunset Fields Overlook flagged me down. She told me a tale of how she and a recent gentleman acquaintance had gone hiking to Apple Orchard Falls. They decided to take a different route back when they became confused and darkness overcame them. The woman decided to find a comfortable location and wait out the night rather than try to hike around in the dark. The man insisted on continuing to get help. The man took off, and the woman cuddled against a tree for what she described as a rather snug night. Once daylight returned, she was able to find the trail and quite easily hiked her way back to their car.

We began searching for the missing man. He was found not far from where he had left the trail and followed a drainage uphill past where his car was parked. He finally became exhausted and spent the night under a rock ledge about thirty feet from a mountain stream. It must have been a slow news day, because by the time one of our rangers escorted him out to the parking area, there was a satellite truck from a local television station. During the on-scene live broadcast, the recently found lost hiker told a dramatic story of survival in the wilderness, including the fact that he had to drink his own urine to stay alive. We all just turned and walked away to laugh. They should have interviewed the woman, who, by the way, told me this was her last outing with this guy.

I received a telephone call at home at three o'clock one morning from the Nelson County dispatcher, who informed me that two University of Virginia students were lost on Humpback Rocks. The dispatcher gave me their cell phone number, and I called them. They had started their hike just before midnight, wanting to see the night view from Humpback Rocks. The moon was up, and they did not take any flashlights. While they enjoying the view, the moon went down, and things went dark. In attempting to find their way back down the mountain, they got off the trail and had been wandering around in the dark for over an hour and wanted us to come get them. It was a warm, dry night; neither had any health problems or concerns, and after questioning them I determined that the area they were most likely in was riddled with dangerous rock formations and cliffs. I advised them that we could not get to them before daylight, so the safest thing for them to do was to find a comfortable spot and wait until daylight.

About twenty minutes later, I got another call from the county dispatcher saying that the lost duo wanted me to call them back. Again they wanted someone to come and rescue them. They told me a pack of coyotes were circling them, and they were afraid they were going to be attacked. I informed them that although it was true we had several sightings of coyotes in the area, they did not hunt in packs and would be afraid of any humans. I again returned to bed.

A half hour later the phone rang again. This time, it was one of the park's volunteers. He had been sitting up, listening to his scanner, and wanted to know if I was aware of a major search going on at Humpback Rocks. I told him what had transpired so far as to the two lost students. He informed me that three fire departments, two rescue squads, and a state police helicopter were en-route to search for two lost UVA students. They had not gotten what they wanted from me, so they had called the Virginia State Police, who sent a trooper to the trail head. He had in turn ordered the world to respond. I finally got up for the last time, got dressed, and headed north to find out what was going on.

When I arrived, the parking area was jammed full of emergency vehicles, and a helicopter with a spotlight was circling over the mountain. As I pulled in, three all-terrain vehicles took off up the Appalachian Trail, spinning gravel. I noted a state trooper sitting in his vehicle, talking on his radio. I was pretty worked up, and I thought my adrenalin was pumping a bit too hard until I met the state police first sergeant that pulled in behind me. He exited his vehicle spouting, "Who the hell ordered that helicopter?" I was quick to inform him that the trooper in the car had made that call, not the park service. It turns out that the sergeant had also spoken by phone to the lost students and told them to sit tight until morning. Once the sergeant and I got each other calmed down, we began to get the situation under some level of control.

The helicopter kept circling and thought they had sighted the students, but each time they came back around they lost them again, finding them in another spot. We made contact with the students by phone and told them to stay in one spot so we could find them.

It was not until about 6:30 a.m. before several firefighters on the ground made visual contact with them. When they were sighted, the students were walking away from their rescuers in the opposite direction from the parking area where we all were waiting. Eventually, they were brought out to our vehicles at about 7:30 a.m. The first thing I said to them was that I had told them earlier that morning that they would not get out before daylight and to turn around and look at the recently risen sun. During the search debriefing, we found that no matter how many people told them to stay put, they had been moving all night and even while the helicopter was looking for them. They said they thought they could still find their way out. I was a bit frustrated thinking about the hundreds of man hours that ended up being expended and thousands of dollars it had cost the state of Virginia to run the helicopter. I told them both that I had thought the University of Virginia was highly competitive and difficult to get into, and I was going to contact the admissions department to find out how the two of them could slip through these rigorous standards.

Another incident that sticks in my mind involved two couples from Waynesboro, Virginia, who decided to hike to Humpback Rocks one summer night. Waynesboro is only fifteen miles from the trail head, and all these folks grew up in this area. The two young men had an urge to show the girls and each other how fast they could hike to the top of the steep and rugged mile and a half trail. They made it to the top and waited for an hour, but the girls never showed up. Then they hiked back down the trail to their car and still saw no sign of the girls. Again, they hiked to the top of the trail and back, with still no sign of the girls. At this point they got on a CB radio and called for help. By the time the report got to the Blue Ridge Parkway dispatcher and I arrived at the scene, there were more than one hundred people with CB radios that were running at high speed up and down the road, and who knows how many had headed into the woods trying to find the girls. Rumors had been spread via CB radio that the girls may have been kidnapped or attacked by bears. I had to call more park rangers out just to get the crowd under control. Several people had obviously been drinking, and we found a few carrying firearms for the alleged kidnappers or vicious bears that had supposedly taken the girls. It took couple of hours to get the situation under control.

We were finally able to organize several search teams and got them into the woods, covering the trails in the area where the girls were supposed to have been. One of the techniques used by the searchers is what is referred to as "attraction." This involves stopping periodically and calling the missing person's name and then listening for a response. This technique was used throughout the area with no results.

Just after daylight, the two missing women were found coming out of the woods onto the Blue Ridge Parkway about a half mile south of the trail head. During the post-search debriefing, I was able to piece together that they had been following the two men up the trail when they got off on one of the social trails leaving the main designated trail. Eventually, they lost the trail and tried to find their way in the dark traveling cross-country. Where they ended up was in an area between the main trail and the Blue Ridge Parkway. This appeared to be very close to where we had searchers the night before walking the trail and calling their names. I asked if they had heard the searchers calling. They both said they had indeed heard the shouting but thought it was wild animals. I then asked them how they explained the animals knowing their names. The response was that they did not think of that.

So how can you prevent these situations from happening to you? The main message we tried to get across to visitors include these:

- Never hike alone.

- Stay together as a group.

- The group should only move as fast as the slowest member.

- Tell someone where you are going and when you plan to return.

- Take adequate drinking water for everyone. This even applies on short hikes of an hour or more.

- Carry gear and supplies and be prepared for weather changes.

- Should you get separated or lost, sit down and stay put. This makes it much easier for to find you. We always taught school children when lost to "hug a tree" and stay in place.

- Remember that cell phones are helpful, but they do not let someone zero in on your location. You would be surprised how many people think this is the way it works.

The Long Search

In 1987, Mark Powell was working his first summer season with the national park service. He was hired at Shenandoah National Park as a fee collector at the Rockfish Gap Entrance Station. Rockfish Gap is the point at the southern end of Shenandoah where the Skyline Drive joins the Blue Ridge Parkway. Mark was well liked by his fellow employees and thought to be doing an excellent job working with the public. In fact, he was so well thought of that he was promoted after only a month to an interpretive park ranger job at Loft Mountain Campground. In this position, he was taking visitors on guided walks and conducting evening campfire programs, sharing his love of the outdoors and the glories of nature found in Shenandoah National Park. Just a couple of years earlier, this devotion to the outdoors had driven him to hike the entire 2,000 mile length of the Appalachian Trail, earning the title of "Through Hiker." The Appalachian Trail parallels the Blue Ridge Parkway and Skyline Drive through this area, and it passes near the Loft Mountain Campground. These were some of the reasons that Mark had chosen Shenandoah National Park to work in.

Everything appeared to be going well and up and coming in Mark Powell's life. He socialized with his fellow seasonal employees, and one young lady even started showing more interest in Mark than the others. She invited Mark to go with her to Washington, D.C., on their days off. On the arranged date,

Mark never showed up at their planned meeting place. His car was not at his park residence during his two days off. On the third day, he did not show up for work, and his car was still not at his residence. No one in the park had heard from him. This was highly unusual for Mark, and people began to worry. By Saturday these concerns lead to a supervisory ranger from Shenandoah contacting Mark's parents at this home in Pennsylvania. His parents' concern was apparent from the first second, once they knew Mark was missing. What no one in the park service knew until that point was the Mark Powell had been fighting depression and mental illness since his early teens. He had attempted suicide less than a year before and spent six months in a mental health facility. The key seemed to be that he had difficulty dealing with success. His last suicide attempt had followed his graduation from college.

At that time, I was working as the James River district ranger for the Blue Ridge Parkway, which included the park's junction with Shenandoah National Park. It was an unusual year for me, since all my full-time rangers had transferred out of the park within two months of each other. I entered the busiest season of the year with no permanent full-time staff, only three experienced returning temporary employees, and eight new seasonal employees who had never worked with the park service before. I was working seven days a week, and a short day was twelve hours. The Blue Ridge Parkway's managers at headquarters in Asheville, North Carolina, were making no moves to fill the vacant positions due to their ability to save the money from those salaries to benefit the overall park budget. I had seen very little of my family for two months, and in the midst of this, Mark Powell disappeared.

It was August 8, the first Saturday I had taken a day off in over a month, when the phone rang at my house. It was one of my experienced seasonal rangers informing me about the missing employee from Shenandoah National Park, and that his car had been found in the Three Ridge Overlook at mile post thirteen on the Blue Ridge Parkway. This overlook is a popular trail head for the Appalachian Trail. I quickly put on my by now well-worn uniform and responded to the park. Even though the park boundary was only eight miles from my house, I would not return to my home for more than two weeks.

I met with my ranger, Chuck Dininger, and three others from Shenandoah National Park at the Three Ridges Overlook, and there sat Mark Powell's car. At this point, no one had seen him in three days. His backpacking equipment was gone from his park residence, and it was not in his car. It looked like Mark had gone out on the Appalachian Trail, which passed through this overlook. We initially began what are called hasty searches of Appalachian Trail shelters in the area, and checked the hiker logs at each of these sites, which contained no mention and no clues as to where Mark Powell could be.

With the lack of results from these efforts and based on the information from Mark's family, we knew we were going to need more help to find him. By morning we had additional park rangers and other staff from Shenandoah National Park and the Virginia Department of Emergency Services. We also had volunteers from the Appalachian Search and Rescue Conference responding to assist with management of the operation. I contacted the Blue Ridge Parkway dispatcher to request assistance from staff in other districts and administrative support from headquarters, since we would be having lots of people's payrolls to track and procurement of supplies and equipment to support the search effort. I was told that no one was available outside our district, and the administrative division might be able to send someone else to help in the later part of next week. This was the start of a sense of my abandonment and ignorance by the Blue Ridge Parkway's managers. Even though this search operation was centered on the Blue Ridge Parkway, Shenandoah National Park provided full support in personnel, supplies, and equipment.

Park Ranger Hollis Provins from Shenandoah National Park was assigned as the lead investigator for the park service, and he started to interview Mark Powell's fellow employees and family members. A profile of Mark was developed to aid us in establishing where he may have hiked. Based on this information, a large area was identified to set up containment sites where hikers could be interviewed and it could be established as to whether they had seen Mark on the trail. A helicopter was used in an attempt to find some sign of Mark. It quickly became apparent with the summer leafed canopy that the helicopter was useless. Search teams were also sent to locations that Mark had mentioned to friends as favorites along the Appalachian Trail. Still, no clues as to his whereabouts were found.

By August 10 more search teams and volunteers were available, and we began to search along all the trail corridors within the containment sites. By this point we had more than sixty people and five search dog teams involved in the operation. It was beginning to become increasingly complex to keep these people fed, housed, and supplied. I again asked for administrative support from the Blue Ridge Parkway and was told they could not send anyone. Shenandoah National Park sent two incident-experienced folks from their administrative division to help.

At that time the Blue Ridge Parkway maintained a cache of supplies and equipment for wildfires and emergencies in Vinton, Virginia, about two hours away. For two years, no emergency supply or equipment requisitions I had sent to headquarters had been filled. So I requested flashlights, batteries, personnel, and water canteens from the district ranger that oversaw the Vinton area. He sent me one ranger, five canteens, one package of batteries, and three flashlights, not much for the sixty people we needed to outfit. Luckily, several local stores started to let us pick up supplies, with the promise of being paid later.

I also started getting complaints from other districts along the parkway that we were using the park's radios too much and overriding their transmissions. The search management team met and we agreed to order a radio kit through the Interagency Fire System. These kits were available for emergency operations and contained fifty portable radios on an independent radio frequency. Once ordered, these kits normally would arrive at the incident site within twenty-four hours. I completed the proper forms and requested the radio kit through the Blue Ridge Parkway dispatch office. The next day, the radios had still not arrived, and when I called the dispatch office to check on their status, I was told that they had not been ordered because the chief ranger, my supervisor, decided we did not need them. This decision had been made without consulting or advising those running the search. At this point I had been up for three days straight, and my patience was wearing thin. While I was outside fuming and stomping around, one of the dispatchers from Shenandoah National Park that had come south to help us asked what was up. Once I explained the situation, she told me not to worry about it. She then contacted her chief ranger, and the next day the radio kit arrived at our command post.

I felt as if I was caught in the middle of a life-threatening situation. The managers at the headquarters of the Blue Ridge Parkway had no experience with such large-scale and growing emergency operations. They were three hundred miles away and concerned with budgetary and other problems that were closer to home. The search had begun on the Blue Ridge Parkway with the last know point seen being Mark's car in the overlook. Therefore, we had lead responsibility for initiating the search. The search area quickly expanded beyond the boundaries of the park onto U.S. Forest Service lands. The U.S. Forest Service did not have any money budgeted for search and rescue, nor did they have any personnel trained to conduct such operations. Under Virginia state law, the county sheriff's department had jurisdiction for managing searches, and the forest service began by deferring to them. The sheriff's departments had no one trained or experienced in search operations. Both of these agencies in turn deferred to the national park service to continue management of the search within the areas of their responsibility. Forest service employees started to show up on their own and leant their expertise and knowledge of the area and helped with logistical support and transportation of search teams. Most of these people worked on their own, without pay, since their bosses had no way of compensating them.

Their help was invaluable, and they were supported as much as possible by their district ranger.

Shenandoah National Park had a vested interest in that Mark was one of their own, and many of their staff felt an even higher imperative to find him and save his life. These people had not only worked with Mark, they had grown to know and respect him as well as live with him.

My options were to try to step aside, removing the national park service and the Blue Ridge Parkway from maintaining a lead role and turn over the search to less experienced people, or moving ahead, keeping the searchers in the field. Another aspect of continuing in this lead role was that the Blue Ridge Parkway was going to take a big hit on its budget in funding the search. I decided to maintain what we were doing with the hope that Mark would be found at any moment. My training, experience, and gut feeling were not to give up for mere administrative reasons as long as there was a real chance to save Mark Powell. This grated against my supervisors, but they did not step in to stop operations on their own authority.

On the fourth day of the search, the parkway's chief ranger and administrative officer showed up at our command post in the Montebello maintenance area. They were not there to check on the search or lend assistance. They arrived for a previously scheduled housekeeping inspection. At this point we had about a hundred people working out of an area that normally accommodated twelve employees. The chief ranger and administrative officer looked around the area and then took me aside. Rather than ask about the search or offer any help, they wanted to let me know that they realized we had a lot of people working here right now, but they pointed out several housekeeping clean-up jobs they wanted done once the search was over. I felt that the search was an irritation to them and that it disrupted their ordered and scheduled lives. They then got in their car and breezed on down the parkway, heading south.

On August 11 we started implementing grid searches by trained personnel in the area of Maupin Field Shelter on the

Appalachian Trail. This technique is very demanding of time and large numbers of searchers. It was decided to concentrate on this particular area since it was the closest shelter to where Mark's car had been found, and he had mentioned it as a favorite place to several friends. At about noon time a team of searches made up of mostly park rangers from Shenandoah National Park were crawling on their hands and knees through a dense, tangled, mountain laurel thicket impassible to all but rabbits. They were attempting to complete a grid search when they came across what appeared to be an abandoned campsite in a small area that had been cleared of limbs in the center of the twelve-foot-high laurel plants. The thicket was so tangled with heavy, green leaves that a person standing ten feet away could not see the camping equipment and tent left there. Found in this hidden pocket were a tent, backpack, walking stick, grey corduroy slacks, Nike hiking shoes, a red sleeping bag, and a gallon water bottle. All of these items were identified by his roommates as belonging to Mark Powell.

Also found at the site was a bag containing empty Nytol and Unison sleep aid packages. Between them both there were sixty-two pills missing. There was also a receipt, indicating that both packages had been purchased two days before Mark disappeared.

We finally had a solid lead that at least told us what direction Mark had traveled from his car, south on the Appalachian Trail. The campsite was well hidden from view but only a hundred yards from the Maupin Field Shelter, which is quite popular and is visited regularly by long-distance backpackers and day hikers.

Ground and air scent dog teams were assigned to go to this campsite and attempt to pick up a trail or determine a direction of travel. One dog indicated that Mark went back along the trail to his car and then north along the parkway thirteen miles back into Shenandoah National Park. Another dog took the trail toward the Maupin Field Shelter and then lost the scent.

A request was made through the medical examiner's office as to the expected effects on the human body of taking more than sixty-four over-the-counter sleeping pills. The predicted prognosis included a long period of deep sleep followed by a waking to a prolonged confused and disoriented state. Without medical treatment, the kidneys could begin to shut down after seventy-two hours. This information did not bode well for Mark and resulted in an acute heightening in everyone's desire to locate him as quickly as possible. Emotions among the already exhausted searches began to simmer. Several were becoming erratic in their behavior and were forced to go home.

The assistant chief ranger, my direct supervisor, received a telephone call from the superintendent for the Blue Ridge Parkway, wanting to know how long this "search thing" was going to take. There was an important meeting scheduled a few days off for the opening of a new section of the parkway in North Carolina, and he did not want people tied up with this incident and delaying the meeting. This partially explained why I was not getting any support or help from headquarters. The superintendent hoped the search would end by the next day so everyone would be available for the meeting.

While all this analysis was going on, I had left the command post to assist in transporting and guiding the dog teams to the campsite. During my absence the resounding urge to find Mark Powell manifested itself in the decision-making process at the command post. This was compounded by the sudden influx of interest in the search by not only local but the national media. The Virginia Department of Emergency Services decided that we needed more man power and made a request through their state capital political contacts to order military troops. To most of our surprise, the next morning a hundred soldiers from Fort Lee, Virginia, showed up. Although the gesture was positive, these were people with no search training or experience, no transportation, no logistical support, and who were demanding to be put up in hotels and fed in restaurants. According to their commanding officer, this was the deal worked out with the state, and that the park service would pay for it.

At this point, we still did not have any administrative support from the Blue Ridge Parkway's headquarters to help coordinate and pay any of the bills piling up. I kept approving expenses for supplies that were necessary to keep the operation going. On the morning of August 13 we were trying to organize, assign, and provide logistical support for almost two hundred people. None of our district staff had received a break and were nearing exhaustion, trying to keep up with the demands of such a large operation that we did not have the resources to support. Again I made a request for management, logistical, and administrative assistance. I received no response.

Later that morning I once again had to assist in getting the dog teams out to their assigned locations. The rugged mountainous terrain was wearing out dogs and handlers at an amazing rate. We kept receiving new teams each day, and many were not familiar with the area.

During the afternoon a search team of park rangers found what would be the second most important clue as to Mark Powell's whereabouts. Approximately one mile south of the Maupin Field Shelter, they had found what looked like a human footprint on a muddy bank of Campbell Creek. It was theorized that Mark may have left his hidden campsite in his stocking feet, since his Nike hiking boots had been found with the rest of his gear. Although other areas of search were not abandoned, the decision was made to make a stronger effort down the drainage from this location.

While I was gone that morning, the equipment cache controlling district ranger from Vinton arrived to see what was going on. When I returned, my fellow district ranger had left after spending an hour and a half at the command post. To my surprise, I received a call from our dispatch office to inform me that the superintendent had ordered a Type 1 Wildland Fire Management Team to respond and take over the search. Apparently the visiting district ranger had called the superintendent and told him everything was going to hell and that we needed help. The superintendent must have taken the other district ranger's word over mine for the need of assistance because all kinds of help started showing up five days after I had requested it. This was a good decision, but I felt defeated and betrayed in the way it came about.

The Powell Search now became a national level incident that was to be watched very carefully at many levels. It also became unique because Type 1 Wildfire Management Teams had been developed under the Incident Command System to handle major forest fires that mainly occurred in the west. They were experienced in running fire operations that involved thousands of personnel and millions of acres each year. This was the first time this training and experience was going to be applied to a nonfire search operation. So as the team arrived, it was apparent that although they had lots of experience with fire operations and could plan ahead for that, they had none in searches. Quickly identifying this deficiency and knowing that the outcome of this operation could affect the use of these teams in future nonfire incidents, the national park service at the Washington headquarters level assigned two highly experienced park rangers to the team.

By August 14 the Incident Management Team was in place. The main core of the Fire Team organized and ran the logistics of the operation while the experienced rangers ran the search operations and assisted in directing planning.

As part of the resources that arrived with the management team were several experienced man trackers from the Great Smokey Mountains National Park. On the morning of August 14 they went to the location where the footprint had been found the day before. They confirmed that it was made by a human wearing a sock and led downstream. They were able to follow the trail a short distance through the drainage, but then lost it in the thick leaves and underbrush.

At this point I had still not made it home. I had only two changes of clothes from the emergency stash in my office in seven days and had been catching at the most two hours of sleep at a time in my truck or on the ground in a sleeping bag behind the command post. I was only able to talk to my wife briefly three or four times by phone. We only had two phone lines, and they were kept busy at all times, so it was difficult to even make this contact. Remember, in 1987 we did not have cell phones, and the nearest pay phone was almost as far as my house from the command post at Montebello, Virginia. On the afternoon of the August 14, my wife, Linda, and four-year-old son, Brian, showed up looking for me. What I had not even considered was the effect of this search on my own family. Brian had been watching television and seen news reports about the search for a lost park ranger. That morning he had turned to Linda and asked, "Is my daddy dead?" At that point she wisely packed him in the car and drove the ten miles to Montebello to verify that I was still alive and kicking. I still treasure the photograph that shows me sitting on the edge of a picnic table talking to several questioning people. Behind me seated on the table is a four-year-old boy with a huge grin on his face. That photo told me what an impact and stress this experience was placing on my loved ones. Unfortunately, in many ways, it was just beginning.

My son Brian smiling behind my back after my wife brought him to our Command Post to prove I was still alive.

Another important part of the search operation had centered on dealing with the media. This was handled by a team working as public information officers under the incident commander. They had distributed basic information and photos to numerous local and national news outlets, and Mark's photo had been run in newspapers and TV stations for days. On August 15 the command post received a telephone call from James Fritz of Richmond, Virginia. His call was transferred to one of the staff of investigators assigned to the search, who told the following story. On Friday, August 7 Fritz and his eight-year-old son had been hiking on the Mau-Har Trail. This is a trail that runs from the Maupin Field Shelter on the Appalachian Trail paralleling the Campbell's Creek drainage south and rejoining the Appalachian Trail approximately five miles south. While hiking at a high point of the Trail after it leaves Campbell's Creek and climbs back toward the Appalachian Trail, they came across a young man hiking southbound. When they called out a greeting to him, he did not respond and walked right past them like he did not see them. Fritz had also thought it was unusual that the hiker was not wearing boots but had the remnants of tattered socks on his feet. They also remembered that the hiker's legs were badly scratched with dried blood, and he had a large, fresh-looking raspberry on his right thigh. Fritz and his son did not realize that they had most likely become the last people known to see Mark Powell until they returned home from their camping trip on August 15 and saw his photo on the evening news.

All search efforts then became focused on the area south of the location where Fritz had met Mark. This sighting was to become our last concrete clue as to Mark's location. By August 17 time had run over the limit of survivability, based on the drugs he had apparently induced. The description by Fritz of Mark's appearance and lack of response were indicative of the symptoms from the number of over-the-counter sleeping aids predicted by our consulting physicians. No one gave up at this point, and the search operation continued with as many as five hundred personnel until August 18 when we started to scale back on the number of people involved. Eventually we dwindled down to an investigative team to follow up on any leads and a few personnel to man containment stations continuing to interview hikers for new information.

On August 30 we received a report that two men illegally digging ginseng plants on U.S. Forest Service lands within our search area had found a partially decomposed body. I responded to the location along with an investigator from the state police and several members of the local rescue squads. We found the body of a human that was decomposed beyond recognition. The clothing that was left matched what was assumed to be worn by Mark Powell. In fact, the tee shirt we found looked exactly like the one he was wearing in the photo that had been distributed to the media and bulletin boards throughout the area.

He was found in the bed of a deeply cut dry drainage. On one side of the drainage was a steep rock cleft. The other side was a steep bank, and where he laid was in a dry hole which during wet times was a pool at the base of an eight-foot water fall. On the rocks at the top of the dry waterfall sat two tattered, rag wool socks, neatly placed side by side. There were no shoes on the victim. This spot was about two hundred yards down the slope from the Mau-Har Trail and not far from where Fritz had reported meeting the distressed young hiker.

There was no doubt in our minds that we had found Mark. It was confirmed two days later by the medical examiner matching dental records.

The area where Mark was found had been covered numerous times by not only human searchers but air scent search dogs with no results. The only explanation is that the ginseng hunter had stepped up on the log left by a fallen tree looking over the forest floor for plants and just happened to look into this specific hole and see the green of Mark's tee shirt. The scent must have been held down in the hole during the search by the heavy humidity that hung in the drainage and prevented the dogs from alerting us to Mark's presence.

On September 4 the Virginia Medical Examiner's office

completed their autopsy and the final report as to the cause of Mark Powell's death. His death was the result of ingesting the over-the-counter sleeping aids. This resulted in an overdose of diphenhydramine and acetaminophen This eventually caused coma and death proceeded by agitation, blurred vision due to enlarged pupils, confusion, delirium, incoherence, movement problems, and eventually convulsions, and coma. Once in a coma, vital organs started to shut down. They were unable to estimate the time of death due to the condition of the body. It was theorized that Mark came to this final resting place not long after being seen by the Fritzes.

Although this was a tragic ending to a herculean effort by more than five hundred people, at least the mystery was solved, and some closure was made for Mark's family and fellow employees. There were obvious signs of grief and failure compounded by fatigue and stress among most participants in the search. At that time there was a relatively new process to aid employees and volunteers in dealing with such strain. This is referred to as critical incident stress debriefing. The process makes use of interviews by both professional and peer counselors and allows for participants to vent and bring out any concerns or stresses they are experiencing.

I contacted the chief ranger of the Blue Ridge Parkway and recommended this process be made available for our employees. I was told that they had already been contacted about starting the process and decided it was a waste of time. We had already spent so much money on the search that they could not see spending any more. I then spoke with the assistant chief ranger at Shenandoah National Park, and they offered to fund the stress debriefing for us.

Our stress debriefing session was held at the Montebello maintenance area on the Blue Ridge Parkway. Disappointingly, not many employees showed up after hearing that park management had said it was a waste of time. The group that did attend sat and spoke about the search quite openly. I thought I had been very quiet during the session. Once we ended, two members of the debriefing team asked to speak with me. Both were professional counselors. They surprised me by saying that they were very concerned about me. They asked several questions and both thought that I was showing signs of clinical depression and that I should seek immediate professional help. I knew I was stressed and exhausted, and this scared me, but apparently not enough since I never followed through on their recommendation. I did not realize for many years how I paid for this. My wife told me later that I became very withdrawn and noncommunicative for several years after this event. My relationship with my wife and son suffered for it. I am fortunate that my wife stayed with me through this time and greatly helped me make it to the other side.

The search for Mark Powell involved more than five hundred employees and volunteers that worked almost eighty thousand hours. Costs were in excess of $500,000.

However, my time with the Powell Search, as it was known, was still not over.

It was determined at the national park service and U.S. Forest Service headquarters in Washington, D.C., that a board of review was needed to examine what went right and what went wrong during this major event. They wanted to examine these issues due to the expenditure of funds and the first-time use of the fire management team on a nonwildfire incident. Since all the search incident records were at my office (the Blue Ridge Parkway had no computers at this time in field offices, so the entire record was on paper, either typed or handwritten), and I was the one manager involved from start to finish, it would be my job to present the chronological events of the search to the board.

I spent two weeks organizing a four-foot stack of documentation and writing summaries of what happened each day. I prepared maps on overhead transparencies to illustrate the chronological progress of the search.

The board was to meet in Asheville, North Carolina, the hometown of the Blue Ridge Parkway's headquarters. Attendees included the chief ranger, protection specialist, and administrative officer from the Blue Ridge Parkway, the head for Search and Rescue and Emergency Services for the park service, and several other representatives from the national park service and U.S. Forest Service regional offices in Atlanta, Georgia. It was a pretty high-powered and intimidating group. I spent one long day presenting the chronological story of the search for Mark Powell. I was grilled with questions as the board members thought of them. My one positive experience with this was that very early into the procedure it became apparent to everyone else, experts in their fields, that the representatives from the Blue Ridge Parkway's management team had no idea what they were talking about and asked very unprofessional questions. I started to notice that each time they tried to interject themselves, the others would just roll their eyes.

Once the review was over, the top official from the U.S. Forest Service took me aside and told me that he thought I did an incredible job, he was impressed, and that anytime I wanted a job with the forest service to give him a call.

The chief of search and rescue and emergency services for the national park service also congratulated me for doing such a great job and for keeping the operation from getting out of control. He thought I had performed very professionally.

The final report reflected both these opinions, and I found some comfort in that. I continued to be ignored and singled out by the management of the Blue Ridge Parkway. Many employees other than myself from the park received achievement awards for their work on this operation. The managers continued to blame me for wasting government funds and time that could have been dedicated to other, more productive activities.

My one consolation continued to be the recognition I received from outside my own park. I was asked by the southeast regional office to conduct incident management training throughout the East Coast using the Powell search as a learning tool. I was requested to assist with search and rescue, fire, and emergency operations throughout the country. I was also offered several job opportunities in other park service areas, which I reluctantly turned down from not wanting to uproot my family and move. I also had the security of knowing that my office was three hundred miles from park headquarters, and that I did not have to deal with the people working there on a regular basis. We entered a period of mutual ignorance of each other. They also did not like the fact that other parks were requesting my assistance with training and management planning. It got to the point where they started denying those requests.

I still had to make it through the rest of the busy visitor season, with my permanent positions vacant. We had to deal with all the regular emergencies and events of day-to-day operations. The park personnel office finally sent out vacancy announcements for the positions in October, after their being vacant for six months. There was a one-month period for applications to be submitted that was followed by two weeks for late postings. I still had not heard anything about a register or list of candidates to hire from by mid-November, so I made a call to the personnel office to check on the hiring status. I was told that the applications still needed to be reviewed and scored by a panel. To do this, they would have to dedicate one person from their office for several days, and that would leave them with only two people to work in personnel. Apparently, this was more critical to the operation of the Park then having only one permanent park ranger in a sixty-five-mile long district for eight months. This again put me in my place and let me know how important what I did was to the management of the park.

The personal effects of this experience devastated my relations with my family. I became despondent, coming home from work and just wanting to sit in front of the television or go to bed. This lasted for several years, and I never realized what was going on. It finally took the life-threatening illness of my wife to make me realize what was going on. It then took over a year to totally break the cycle. As I look back on this search, I still feel a tremble in my abdominal region, and you would detect a bit of a rise in the tone of my voice when discussing it. I did learn an incredible amount about responding to and managing emergencies. My hope is that throughout the rest of my career,

I was able to pass this knowledge on to other park rangers and provide the support and encouragement to let them know that what they do is important.

I have searched my mind and soul for years about these events. Although we faced many challenges, some of which were compounded by the lack of support from inexperienced managers, I know there was nothing we could have done differently to save Mark. Although the Blue Ridge Parkway managers were unsure of how to address this type of incident, the staff and employees of Shenandoah National Park threw their full support and expertise into the effort. There could not have been a more dedicated and focused group of people on the ground and in support and planning roles then in this all-out effort to save Mark. Although I had my own demons to deal with, I felt honored and privileged to have worked with my fellow national park service employees from many parks in addition to my own district in this colossal effort.

There were other decisions made following this search that benefited emergency operations and organization for future emergencies. It was realized that the use of incident management teams could be very effective when used in situations other than wildfires. Training for managing other emergencies was conducted. Teams were then called upon more frequently for situations that resulted in their being prepared to aid in disasters such as Hurricane Andrew in Florida and later Hurricane Katrina in Louisiana.

The national park service established a process allowing a park that was experiencing a major or costly search operation to apply for special funding to cover the costs. This helps a park prevent the destruction of its individual operating budget for a year and not be distracted by making decisions in life-threatening situations based on "How are we going to pay for this?"

The Virginia State Police began a program of training as many of their troopers as possible in the course entitled, "Managing the Search Function." This week-long class was developed by the National Association for Search and Rescue and is the basic training used by the national park service for its park rangers.

I called this story "The Long Search." The physical search for Mark Powell was long and trying, but the emotional impacts on his family and his park service colleagues continued long into all our futures. Mark was a gentle soul who is dearly missed, and that is the true tragedy.

Drugs and Thugs

When I started to work on the Blue Ridge Parkway in 1981, I had the good fortune to have Dean Richardson as my supervisor. I also met Cliff Pendry, who had retired as a park ranger from the same area in 1979. Both of these men were icons among the hundreds of rangers who had worked through the years on the Blue Ridge Parkway. Dean and Cliff had started their careers in the 1940s as two of the earliest rangers assigned there. They were also master storytellers and would keep the attention of a young ranger for hours with their tales of derring-do in the early days of the park. Several of these stories centered on car chases of "moonshiners" transporting illegal alcohol. One of the neighbors to the park where we worked was Junior Johnson, the famous NASCAR race driver. It is a well known fact that Junior developed his driving skills by running illegal liquor when he was young. Dean and Cliff may have chased him a time or two.

After hearing these legendary stories from the ones who lived them, I should not have been surprised by the number and frequency of illegal activities on the Blue Ridge Parkway. Several of the early cases I made for illegal drug possession and drunken driving involved sons and grandsons of those same outlaws chased as far back as the 1940s. As times, conditions, and markets changed, these families with criminal experience simply diversified from moonshining to selling illegal drugs.

Drugs, or what in law enforcement circles are referred to as controlled substances, are very common in national parks. On the Blue Ridge Parkway, we dealt with marijuana, cocaine, heroin, methamphetamines, crack, and large amounts of prescription pain killers. This not only involved the possession and use of these drugs, but their growing, sale, and distribution.

In 1990, I attended a meeting in Roanoke, Virginia, with agents from the Bureau of Alcohol, Tobacco, and Firearms (ATF) and the Drug Enforcement Agency (DEA). These agents briefed us with an overview of their undercover operations being conducted in that area of the state. They were making deals to buy large amounts of drugs, explosives, and illegal firearms. It struck all of us that every agent stated that the bad guys that they were investigating wanted to complete their deals in overlooks on the Blue Ridge Parkway. We were being warned of the presence of these criminals with a high potential for violence so that we would not walk into the middle of an undercover operation. This was an eye-opening revelation for most of the rangers present.

In three overlooks on the Blue Ridge Parkway near Waynesboro, Virginia, we had a serious problem with large gatherings of people partying at night. These parties were a spillover from larger gatherings in public parking lots in Waynesboro. It was not uncommon on weekends for the park maintenance crew to fill a truck with litter each morning just in this relatively small area. Groups of forty or more people would congregate in these overlooks, drinking and using illegal drugs. Soon several assaults involving stabbings and at least one shooting occurred. The situation got so out of hand in Waynesboro that the local government enacted a citywide curfew in all public parking areas after ten o'clock. This pushed even more activity to the Blue Ridge Parkway only five miles away. We were told by several informants that a lot of illegal activities went unreported, and local park neighbors began to complain about the noise and to fear for their lives when driving past these overlooks at night. With our limited staffing it was nearly impossible to get control of this situation.

I instructed the ranger staff to request computer records checks for criminal histories on every individual that was issued a violation notice or written warning in this area. The lists of criminal convictions by most of these people were awe-inspiring. Quite a few had numerous charges of assaults on police officers along with domestic violence and drug convictions. We half-jokingly thought that it must be a badge of honor amongst this population to have the most arrests for assault. This gave us a baseline of information on the type of people we would be dealing with and their potential for violence.

The next step was to have rangers record the license plate numbers of cars parked in the overlooks that did not look like they were there for the view. Over one hundred license plate numbers were given to the regional drug task force to check for any knowledge of the registered owners. We were a bit shocked to learn that 90 percent of those checked had criminal histories, the majority of which involved violence and illegal drugs. Several were reputed to be local drug dealers.

Struggling for a solution, I contact several local and state agencies, finding that they too had concerns about illegal activities in this area. The problem was that they did not have enough officers to divert them from duties outside their regular jurisdictional responsibilities.

I worked with Skip Wissinger from Shenandoah National Park to develop a plan to conduct a traffic check point on the Blue Ridge Parkway, utilizing officers from two sheriff's departments, the state police, and additional rangers from Shenandoah National Park, our neighbor to the north. The first Friday night we checked over 1,200 cars in two hours. Eight drunken driving arrests were made, ten illegal firearms were confiscated, including several from convicted felons, in addition to large amounts of illegal drugs. In total, twenty arrests were made that night. We conducted these joint operations over a two-month period. By the end of the summer we were checking as few as a hundred cars in one evening. The word had gotten out that this was not the place to conduct open illegal activities.

We thought the situation was under control until one day when I received a telephone call from a detective in Waynes- boro. He wanted to meet with me to discuss some activities in the park. He informed me that his department was running several undercover officers and informants. Almost every drug deal that they made was conducted on the Blue Ridge Parkway. That was the only place the dealers felt safe. They estimated that more than $1 million had changed hands in the Rockfish Valley Overlook in the last six months.

At that time I only had myself and one other ranger work- ing in our district. I knew I was going to need help if we had any chance of getting this situation under control. It was only a matter of time before some innocent park visitor drove into the middle of one of these drug deals. Another informant contacted the Waynesboro Police Department and told a tale of a drug dealer from New Jersey that was using this same overlook to distribute to locals. This dealer was in the Rockfish Valley Over- look one night with the informant when a park ranger patrol vehicle drove through. The informant asked what they should do if the ranger stopped to check them. The dealer pointed to a sawed-off shotgun between the seats and said that was not a problem. If the ranger stopped, the dealer said, "I'll just blow him away."

The Waynesboro Police Department was willing to assist us all they could, but their chief was reluctant to dedicate re- sources to criminal activity outside their jurisdictional respon- sibility. A detective from Waynesboro was able to arrange a meeting with an agent from the DEA, but she said that they would not be able to get involved unless we actually showed them a large amount of cocaine that we had taken. They would not step in to help unless the case was already made. That was another dead end.

A month later the national park service's southeast regional law enforcement specialist from Atlanta was visiting the park to teach a training course. During a break in class, I was able to corner him and give him a quick rundown on our situation. He seemed interested and stayed an extra day to meet with representatives from several local agencies to assess the situation. He determined that he should assist by providing special law enforcement funding that would enable us to detail extra park rangers from other areas and to pay for travel and overtime. I was instructed on how to apply for the funding and given several examples of applications that were approved in the past. I put together all this information and submitted it through the Blue Ridge Parkway chief ranger for his signature, since the official request had to originate from him. I discussed the request with the chief and assumed that the process would begin. When I had heard no reply for more than a month, I called the regional law enforcement specialist. He told me that he had never received the application, and that he was disappointed that we had not followed up on this investigation. I immediately called the chief ranger and in wonderment was told that he had not forwarded the request for funding since he felt we should not get involved in such serious law enforcement investigations. He felt that was the job of the DEA, not us.

The illegal activities continued, and my fear of an innocent visitor getting hurt or worse prevailed. Our only recourse was to keep a close watch on the area in question and try to make it uncomfortable for drug dealers. I was able to enlist the assistance of park rangers from Shenandoah National Park to assist us in presenting a presence of uniformed rangers in the overlooks. Any cars that were parked after dark were checked and the drivers were asked to present operator's permits. Quite a few minor violation notices were written for charges such as alcohol and small amounts of drugs. Eventually word got back to the Waynesboro police that the drug dealers were feeling too uncomfortable to conduct business on the parkway. I know we were not able to put an end to such activities, but we temporarily forced it to either relocate or become much less open.

Illegal drug use and its effects show up in different ways within our parks. In 1998, we received a report around midnight to the Blue Ridge Parkway dispatch office from the Augusta County sheriff's department of a woman lost on the Appalachian Trail near Rockfish Gap. Once again I tried to shake the sleep from my near consciousness and responded to that area. Upon my arrival I noted a sheriff department's detective off to the side, away from the other officers, interviewing a man who appeared agitated. He was wearing a torn and filthy tee shirt that may have once been white, dirty, faded blue jeans, and mud-splattered tennis shoes. Although his dark, stringy hair hung in his face, I could see his eyes looking wide, like they were on fire as his entire body was twitching with overactive nervousness. I could tell this guy was hiding something just from observing his mannerisms.

This turned out to be the reporting party. He told us that he and his girlfriend were hiking on the Appalachian Trail, which parallels the Blue Ridge Parkway through this area, when they became separated. He spun a story about how they had started at a location to the north in Shenandoah National Park and that his girlfriend was hiking in bare feet. I knew the location he gave us in Shenandoah was about thirty miles north of where we were meeting, and he had lost his girlfriend south of there at Rockfish Gap. I also noted that he was not dressed in hiking clothes or shoes; he had no pack or gear that would normally be taken on an all-day, long-distance trek.

The detective took me aside and explained that there was a bit more to the situation. He informed me that not only was this guy a suspected drug dealer, but also a main suspect in the murder of a woman and her child in Augusta County. The man reporting the loss of this girlfriend had met the murder victim, moved in with her, and got her hooked on methamphetamines. The woman and her daughter had been found murdered in their mobile home. The nervously twitching subject across the hood of the car from us had then moved in with the woman he was reporting missing and had gotten her hooked on meth. At this point, we suspected that we might be searching for a body and crime scene.

Tracking dogs and additional law enforcement officers were called to assist. We knew we could not use volunteers for this search since a serious crime was suspected. Unfortunately, due to other incidents going on at the same time, there were not many people available to help. Even I could only contact one other park ranger to respond, and he was over an hour away.

An Appalachian trail shelter for backpackers was located about six miles south on the trail, and there were normally people camping there this time of year. No one else at the scene knew how to find the shelter nor was in physical shape to hike in and out, so I volunteered. I thought it would be a waste of time, since this guy's story seemed pretty farfetched, but we could not afford to ignore it. So I hiked the two miles into the Paul Wolfe Trail Shelter. Once there I found three groups of hikers sleeping in the shelter and tents through the area. Several informed me that a couple of hours earlier a woman had come down the trail from the north, took a drink from the stream, and when they attempted to talk to her, she ran back north on the trail. I asked if they had noticed anything unusual about her and one person responded, "Yeah, as a matter of fact she was in bare feet, and I thought that was pretty weird." Unbelievably, it sounded like we had actually been told at least part of the real story.

In the meantime, a search dog and team had been sent south on the Appalachian Trail seven miles north of me. The sheriff's department had lost radio contact with them once they were an hour down the trail. With the report of the woman heading back north on the trail and a missing dog team, I started to hike all the way along the rocky and at times steep trail the seven miles to Rockfish Gap. It took me several hours and some stumbling in the dark to work my way through, stopping to look for signs of the missing woman and the dog team. Just before dawn I came out on the Blue Ridge Parkway at Rockfish Gap. The dog team had turned around and returned a half hour before me with both man and beast exhausted.

We then decided to set up a command post at the Humpback Rocks Visitor Center and develop a new plan. Because we were still concerned that we would find a crime scene, we could only make use of law enforcement officers for searchers.

About this time an Augusta County deputy pulled into an overlook to walk around and try to wake up. When he looked down below the overlook in the lightening dawn, he thought he saw a person or body in the brush. As he started down the bank to check it out, a woman jumped up and ran away from him. At first startled, the deputy took off after her, catching her and knocking her down. He dragged her kicking and screaming back to the overlook and called for assistance.

When I arrived, she was seated in the backseat of the deputy's car, screaming and cursing. Her clothes were in tatters, her hair matted and full of leaves and twigs. I looked in the car and also saw that she was barefooted with both feet torn into bloody pulps. When I looked at her face, I could swear her head was going to spin around like a scene from *The Exorcist*. She looked up at me through the rear seat window with hatred and violence.

It was quite obvious that she was strung out on meth. She looked nothing like the driver's license photos the sheriff's department was able to obtain during the night. The use of methamphetamines had taken a strong toll on her physically and mentally. She looked like she had aged twenty years.. We found later that the couple had been using meth and drinking alcohol for seventy-two hours straight.

It was several days later when the whole story finally came to light. Apparently, this couple had run low on money to buy more drugs, so they decided to break into a house and steal what they could sell or trade quickly for meth. A third person drove them to a small subdivision just off the Blue Ridge Parkway and dropped them off. As they approached the rear of what appeared to be vacant house, an outside light came on, drowning their drug-fogged minds in brilliant retina-burning illumination. They panicked, ran into the woods, and became separated in the dark. The woman had seen and heard us searching for her the night before, but hid from us for fear of getting her boyfriend in trouble. I hope she finally figured out that this guy was nothing but trouble. Both of them ended up in the county jail, under a variety of charges.

In 1984, I was working on the Blue Ridge Parkway in North

Carolina based out of an office near the town of Spruce Pine. A big item in the news was the escape from a prison in Tennessee of four convicts who had killed a guard and then several other people along their escape route to the east. They had stolen several cars and firearms from homes of their victims. Law enforcement agencies all over the region were mounting a massive manhunt. I asked my supervisor if we should be out looking for these criminals and was told that there was no way they would be on the Blue Ridge Parkway.

The next day a North Carolina state trooper was shot on Interstate 40 approximately twenty miles from our office. He had stopped a car for speeding, not knowing that it was recently stolen and contained the four escaped convicts.

On a state road intersecting the Blue Ridge Parkway, I found a team of state troopers conducting a traffic check point. I called my supervisor and was instructed not to stop vehicles traveling in the park since that would inconvenience visitors and "besides, they wouldn't be on in the park." So I assisted the state troopers on the state road for eight hours or so.

As is common when park rangers live in national parks, my supervisor was our next door neighbor. The next day I was in my yard with my one-year-old son when I saw my supervisor at his house going through the trunk of his patrol car. I could tell that he was very frustrated and was throwing things right and left onto the ground. Trying to be helpful I asked, "Dave, what are you looking for?"

"I'm trying to find my gun belt."

"Oh, okay, I guess I'll see you later," I said. I figured that if he could not find his gun belt I would be of little help.

Ten minutes or so later, I went back outside and noted that Dave was still going through his trunk. I could see his gun belt on the ground next to him. "What are you looking for now?"

"This is all your fault."

Now I knew I should have stayed inside minding my own business.

"I'm looking for my shotgun," Dave said.

I had never seen Dave with a shotgun in his car and I was pretty sure it was locked up in the gun cabinet in the office. "What's going on?," I asked.

"Evidently, you took it upon yourself to help the state police yesterday. Now they are making a formal request for us to help them look for those escapees. It is a waste of our time. You know those guys won't be in the park."

I took a deep breath and asked Dave if he wanted me to go with him. He jumped at this offer, and we spent eight hours manning another traffic check point. We never did see those escapees.

The next day, however, the state police did see them when a citizen reported some suspicious activity around an abandoned farm house ten miles outside the park. A major gun battle ensued, resulting in another officer being wounded and two of the escapees being killed.

During their brief crime spree, the escapees had killed five people and wounded two police officers. The two surviving and wounded escapees were interviewed intensely in an attempt to trace their route to determine whether there were more unknown victims out there. There were four days that were not accounted for by crimes or sighting of the criminals. One of the escapees finally admitted that they had spent the entire four days on the Blue Ridge Parkway between Asheville and Mount Mitchell in North Carolina. During that time they had slept in overlooks in one of their many stolen cars.

When I received this information, I was astounded and convinced that if one of our park rangers, perhaps even myself, had stopped to check on that car in an overlook we would have met the same attack as the trooper who was shot on the Interstate. When I spoke to my supervisor about this, his only response was, "Naw, that wouldn't happen in the park."

It was not to be until Fathers Day in 1998 that park ranger, Joe Kolodski, was shot down in the line of duty on the Blue Ridge Parkway. It was this murder of one of our own that finally brought home to many that, yes, it could happen on the Blue Ridge Parkway.

Inherent Dangers

Early in my career I was young and full of myself, never thinking that any serious injury could occur to me. It was partly the typical youthful sense of immortality combined with confidence in my ability and training. As I became more mature, experienced, and responsible for other employees, I began to realize that this was mostly false bravado and that I was truly fortunate that I survived that time in my life. It was common to work at night alone with no way of summoning help, even if it was available. There was no dispatcher to listen to my one-frequency radio. There were no cell phones yet, and pay phones were few and normally nonexistent in remote areas. Under these conditions I still stopped violators, arrested drunks, and confronted armed criminals. As I look back on thirty years ago, I now believe what was the norm was just plain stupid.

Later in my career, I became a supervisor responsible for other park rangers' lives. I found these lives much harder to risk than I had my own. I did not want them to be working alone nor without radio communications and a cell phone to summon help. This attitude was the result of my own experiences, the development of more professional expectations, and the impression that the potential for violence was becoming much more prevalent. More and more simple contacts made with the public for very minor violations were quickly escalating and at times coming close to blows. A person being asked to place their pet on a leash was resulting in a backlash of accusations and incriminations of the park ranger, the government, and society in general. Individuals appeared to be much more interested in their personal space, rights, and opinions then those of society. Any questioning of their actions was becoming an assault on their person and an insult to their integrity.

Others within the national park service began to perceive these same conclusions based on anecdotes from field park rangers and analysis of statistics developed from incident reports coming from the parks. One thesis offered was that physical assaults on park rangers appeared to be increasing. As the result of this concern, several studies were conducted.

The first was through the International Association of Chiefs of Police, who conducted a review of national park service law enforcement programs in 2000 and produced a document of findings entitled *Policing the National Parks: 21st Century Requirements*. This study found that national park rangers suffer from the highest rate of assaults of all federal law enforcement agencies.

A second more academic study was conducted by Dr. Larry Gould of Northern Arizona University in 2004. In Dr. Gould's report. entitled *Analysis of Assaults on National Park Rangers 1997 to 2003*, he states, "The short and accurate answer is that NPS rangers are the most likely of federal law enforcement employees to be assaulted."

There are many theories as to why national park rangers are so frequently victims of assault. Examples include the following:

Park rangers most often work alone in remote areas with little or no backup available. This knowledge results in suspects feeling more confident in resorting to violence.

Park rangers are by nature multi-taskers expected to not only be able to handle law enforcement situations but fight fires, search for lost hikers, provide emergency medical care, do technical rescue work, and all other duties assigned. Each of these functions also has its own inherent dangers to face. This multi-functioning may cause confusion or delay in decision making and reactions to quickly developing situations with high potential for violence.

Law enforcement commissioned rangers are ultimately supervised, managed, and judged by people with no law enforcement experience or authority. These individuals have never been placed in a potentially life-threatening situation where the outcome will result from a split-second decision. A park ranger's concern over a possible negative judgment of their actions may also result in a slowed reaction or decision for escalation of force to protect themselves or others.

National park rangers differ from other federal agencies in that they provide full-service law enforcement and emergency response. Most agencies have much more specific areas of responsibility and do not get involved in everyday incidents that are high risk, such as stopping vehicles, responding to domestic disturbances, and dealing with people under the influence of alcohol or drugs.

Whatever the reasons, the real potential for danger and violence exists every day in the career of a national park ranger. Those still working in our national parks and the public need to be aware of these conditions and provide for a safe work environment for park rangers and other park employees.

Based on experience and an examination of past incidents, today's national park rangers need to be assured of the importance and benefit of their work. There should be constant validation and support from managers and the public for the protection of life and resources in our national parks. Visitors and employees deserve a high level of protection provided by highly trained, well-equipped, and adequately staffed park rangers. Numerous internal agency studies have shown that most parks are grossly understaffed in all fields but most evidently in protection positions. A law enforcement assessment was conducted on the Blue Ridge Parkway in 2001. Based on such factors as the resource values to be protected, the number of visitors each year, the number and seriousness of crimes committed and investigated, and the crime rates of surrounding jurisdictions it was determined that there should be a minimal staff of fifty-two law enforcement commissioned park rangers in the park. This level was established to maintain a safe work environment, not to be efficient at preventing crime. At that time, there were a total of twenty-eight rangers in the organization of the Blue Ridge Parkway. As of this writing, that number has remained the same.

This is merely an example from one national park service area and only examining the function of law enforcement. The same conditions exist throughout the United States. As long as the status quo remains, the potential for assaults against and serious injury among park rangers will remain unchanged or will possibly increase.

Sacrifice

After reading these tales of my experiences, it would not be proper to leave the reader with the impression that every day in the life of a national park ranger is full of excitement and without risk. There are less than 1,800 law enforcement park rangers in the entire country. They are spread from Alaska and Hawaii to Maine and the Virgin Islands in almost four hundred separate national park units. That number is less than the number of police officers just in the city of Atlanta, Georgia, alone. During the course of my thirty-two–plus-year career, sixteen of my fellow park rangers died in the line of duty. Their sacrifice reminds all of us of the seriousness and potential for danger in this profession. The loss experienced by their families affects us all.

They should never be forgotten, and their memory held in tribute to their dedication to duty and the national parks in which they served.

On November 26, 1977, **Gregory Burdine** was working on the Colonial Parkway in Virginia when a car passed him going seventeen miles over the speed limit. When he attempted to stop the violator, they took off at a higher rate of speed. Greg lost control of his patrol car during the pursuit and was killed after it struck two trees. Greg was twenty-five years old.

Duane McClure was conducting a patrol by canoe of Yellowstone Lake on May 22, 1980, when he did not return at the end of the day. His overturned canoe was found but his body never recovered. It was presumed after an investigation that he had drowned when the canoe overturned.

Two escaped convicts who had kidnapped a woman shot and killed **Robert McGhee** on May 26, 1990, at Gulf Islands National Seashore. McGhee had stopped the suspects' car after running a stop sign while they were attempting to flee the area after their kidnap victim had escaped. McGhee had no idea that he was stopping armed, escaping felons.

Robert Mahn, Jr. was killed in Yellowstone National Park while on snowmobile patrol. On January 17, 1994, he was found at the bottom of a forty-foot drop-off with his snowmobile on top of him. It is believed that during a period of low visibility and heavy winds, he may have struck a low-lying limb that caused him to lose control of the snowmobile.

On July 3, 1994, **Ryan Waltman** was on kayak patrol on Shoshone Lake in Yellowstone National Park when he failed to make two scheduled radio reports. After a search by air, his kayak was found overturned and his body was later found offshore.

Randy Morgenson was alone on backcountry patrol in Sequoia Kings Canyon National Park in July 1996. when he failed to return to the ranger station. Extended searches of the area found nothing. It was not until July 2001 that Morgenson's remains were located in a remote part of the park. It is believed that he fell while attempting to cross a stream and drowned.

On August 26, 1996, **Michael Beaulieu** was killed in an auto crash while responding to a wildfire in Bryce Canyon National Park.

On June 21, 1998, **Joe Kolodski** started his Fathers Day by taking his wife and three children to church. As he reported to duty later that day at the Great Smokey Mountains National Park, a report came in of a man threatening visitors with a rifle on the Blue Ridge Parkway. Joe responded to the scene to protect others and was shot and killed by the suspect with a rifle bullet that penetrated his protective vest.

On December 12, 1999, **Steve Makuakane-Jarrell** was investigating a report from visitors of a man with aggressive dogs on a trail at Kaloko-Honokohau National Park. A struggle ensued between Makuakane-Jarrell and the suspect, resulting in Steve being shot and killed.

Cale Saffer was killed in an airplane crash while on patrol at Denali National Park on June 19, 2000.

On August 9, 2002, two suspects who had committed multiple murders in Mexico escaped pursuit by crossing the border into Organ Pipe Cactus National Monument. **Kris Eggle** was assisting other agencies in tracking one of the suspects that had left their vehicle. The suspect ambushed, shot, and killed Kris.

On December 20, 2002, **Tom O'Hara** was killed in a plane crash in Katmai National Preserve in Alaska.

Suzanne Roberts was killed while attempting to clear fallen rocks from a roadway in Haleakala National Park. On September 14, 2004, she was leaning over to pick up a rock when a larger rock fell from the cliff above, striking her in the back and head.

Jeff Christiansen was killed in a fall while on backcountry patrol in Rocky Mountain National Park on July 25, 2005.

These National Park Rangers made the ultimate sacrifice to perform their duties to protect our national parks and visitors. Their sense of duty serves as an example to all their fellow park rangers. Their loss is a true tragedy.

Breinigsville, PA USA
04 October 2010
246673BV00001B/5/P